TILE
IDEA BOOK

TILE
IDEA BOOK

ANDREW WORMER

The Taunton Press

To D.C., for never uttering a discouraging word

The Taunton Press

Inspiration for hands-on living®

The Taunton Press, Inc., 63 South Main Street, PO Box 5506, Newtown, CT 06470-5506
e-mail: tp@taunton.com

EDITOR: Stefanie Ramp
JACKET/COVER DESIGN: Jeannet Leendertse
INTERIOR DESIGN: Lori Wendin
LAYOUT: Susan Fazekas
ILLUSTRATOR: Christine Erikson
COVER PHOTOGRAPHERS: Front cover (top row, left to right): © Alise O'Brien; © Linda
Svendsen; © Roger Turk/Northlight Photography Inc.; Photo courtesy of Mark
Samu/www.samustudios.com; (middle row, left to right): Charles Miller, © The Taunton
Press, Inc.; Charles Miller, © The Taunton Press, Inc.; © Lisa Romerein; Photo courtesy of
Mark Samu/www.samustudios.com; Photo courtesy of Winslow Studio, Bozeman, MT;
(bottom row, left to right): © Ken Gutmaker Photography; © Barry Halkin; Photo courtesy
of Mark Samu/www.samustudios.com; © Tim Street-Porter; Back cover (clockwise from top
left): © Roger Turk/Northlight Photography Inc.; © Alise O'Brien; © Tim Street-Porter;
Roe A. Osborn, © The Taunton Press, Inc.

Library of Congress Cataloging-in-Publication Data

Wormer, Andrew.
  Tile idea book / Andrew Wormer.
      p. cm.
  ISBN 1-56158-709-5
  1. Tiles in interior decoration. I. Title.
  NK2115.5.T54W67 2005
  747'.3--dc22

                              2004018523

Printed in the United States of America
10 9 8 7 6 5 4 3 2 1

The following manufacturers/names appearing in *Tile Idea Book* are trademarks:
Corian™, Pébéo Porcelaine 150™

Acknowledgments

I installed my first ceramic-tile floor more than 20 years ago, and each construction project that has involved tile since then has taught me something new about this old material. With the writing of this book, my pace of learning about the range of different kinds of tile options has certainly accelerated, but I'd be the first to acknowledge that I've just barely scratched the surface. Fortunately, I've been able to draw on the expertise and skills of many talented people as I've explored the world of tile and assembled the material for this book.

A number of architects, interior designers, craftspeople, and builders shared insight and information about their work, and while these folks are all credited, I'd also like to give all of them special thanks here for their time and patience. Of course, a book like this wouldn't be possible without great photography, so a special thanks to all of the skilled professionals who contributed their images to this project.

And of course, there is the Taunton team of both old and new faces—Maureen Graney, who got the ball rolling; Stefanie Ramp, who (once again) has made me sound smarter than I am; and Carolyn Mandarano, who fields my every whine and whimper without complaint. Along with all of the others, they've encouraged me from the beginning, looked benignly the other way as I missed deadlines, and then worked their usual magic to help turn a collection of words and images into a cohesive whole. Thanks.

Contents

Introduction

Like my fellow baby boomers, I came of age at a time when it looked like tile was on the verge of becoming an artifact. When the postwar housing boom of the 1950s took off, tile was one building material that seemed to be left behind. Though admired by many for its beauty and durability, few could afford it. Tile choices were limited, and because tile setting was a rather arcane and labor-intensive art practiced by a relatively few skilled tradespeople, installation was expensive. Instead, manufacturers, builders, and homeowners turned to new products, such as vinyl flooring and plastic laminates, that were easier to install and promised the look of tile without the expense.

During the 1960s and '70s, decades characterized by far-out fashions and an almost insatiable thirst for self-expression, the building trades in general—and the tile industry in particular—seemed to be in a continued funk. Tile offerings were limited to bland colors and unimaginative designs, and the lack of skilled installers resulted in some dubious practices that tarnished tile's reputation. The future seemed to belong to plastics, while tile somehow seemed old-fashioned.

Fortunately, the era of platform shoes, bellbottoms, big hair, and bad tile jobs passed. This was about the same time that I graduated from college, became part of the workforce, and bought my first house. Purchased during a time of high interest rates and high oil prices for a sum less than today's average SUV, this house was definitely a fixer-upper. Among the priorities was to add a sunroom with lots of windows and a tile floor to take advantage of passive solar heat gain (not to mention the generous tax incentives available then). Price was the primary factor that I used when selecting that particular tile, and though it was an unremarkable, brown-glazed, Mexican terra cotta look-alike, I was hooked by how well it performed. Ever since then, I've tried to use tile whenever possible, both in my own homes and in projects that I've done for others.

I've made lots of mistakes as I've worked with different kinds of ceramic and stone tile (I'm thinking in particular about a slate floor in a small entryway that I spent an afternoon scrubbing with muriatic acid and a small brush because I neglected to seal the stone before grouting). But luckily for me, the steepest part of my learning curve occurred at the same time that the tile industry began offering new innovations in setting materials, simplified techniques for installing tile, and a steadily increasing variety of ceramic and stone products.

And in another case of good fortune, I discovered Michael Byrne's unambiguously titled *Setting Ceramic Tile* (The Taunton Press, 1987), a resource that gave me the confidence to tackle more ambitious projects with better-looking results. Clearly, here was a guy who knew what he was talking about. I was intrigued not only by the rich variety and traditions of tile and the various techniques for installing it but also by the way that Byrne personified (at least to me) the ideals of craftsmanship: working with your hands, caring about what you do, and using your head as you do it.

I don't think that it's any secret that the resurgence of interest in craftsmanship in general has coincided with the resurgence of

tile, both now and back during the American Arts and Crafts movement in the early part of the twentieth century. I've found that, regardless of its kind, cost, or style, tile is an intriguing finish that wants to be touched and looked at. And while it's challenging to install well, tile offers continuing rewards long after other finishes have grown tired and need replacement.

The ideas presented in this book will help you as you think about the various types of ceramic, stone, glass, and other tiles and consider the wide range of ways that they can be used. Quite simply, there's never been a better time to incorporate tile into your home—variety and availability are up, prices are down. And while tile certainly hasn't lost any of its well-deserved prestige, it truly is a material for everyman, offering both beauty and durability all around the house. Why settle for a finish that has the look of tile when you can have the real thing?

1

Tile Basics

Walking into a tile showroom is a bit like walking into a candy store: With so many good things to choose from, it's hard to know where to begin. But rest assured: Picking out a tile that looks great, is well suited to the use you have in mind, and that will last for years isn't all that complicated.

Tile has been experiencing a renaissance lately. There are literally hundreds of different sizes, types, and styles of tile to choose from. While there are familiar favorites in ceramic and natural stone, there are newcomers too, including tile made of shimmering glass or gleaming metal. And to add even more variety to the mix, there are also look-alikes, such as ceramic tiles that look like stone, concrete tiles that look like ceramic, and composite tiles that look like solid metals.

But choosing tile is only half the fun; tile's design versatility makes it unique among finishing materials. Tile patterns can be bold or subtle and can either emphasize or minimize a room's architectural characteristics.

Where to begin? Just pick out a tile—or tiles—in colors, textures, and styles that appeal to you. Chances are, these won't be the ones you end up with, but they'll provide you with a starting point as you learn which tiles are best suited to your project.

◀ CHOSEN TO COMPLEMENT THE COLORS of an adjoining kitchen, green and beige 4-in.-square tumbled marble tiles set in a diagonal pattern give this fireplace surround a graphic quality that contrasts with the white mantel and emphasizes the fireplace's function as a focal point in the room.

CHOOSING THE RIGHT TILE

In order to select tile that best suits your needs, you should first determine where and how it will be used. The floor of a master bathroom, for example, doesn't see the same kind of traffic that an entryway or mudroom does, thus it doesn't require as durable a tile.

Your family's lifestyle plays an important role in tile selection as well. Busy families with children and pets would be wise to steer toward a low-maintenance floor tile with a color that hides dirt well. Other factors, such as room size and color, should also be considered when selecting the tile most appropriate for your purposes.

▲ THE TILE YOU CHOOSE should reflect your tastes and lifestyle. Here, this dramatic, black-and-white contemporary kitchen has a vaulted ceiling and a playfully formal ceramic floor in an easy-care matte finish that enhances the room's ample natural light and geometric forms.

THE HANDMADE TILES ON THIS FIREPLACE SURROUND were chosen for their three-dimensional quality and the way they suggest the coziness of a down comforter. Combined with the fine detailing of the woodwork, they create a hearth that looks traditional yet doesn't feel austere.

CHOSEN FOR THEIR DEEP-GREEN COLOR and rich veined texture, the marble tiles on this kitchen's countertops and backsplash match the flooring in the adjacent entry and reflect the natural environment found outside the home, which is surrounded by a spruce forest on Maine's Casco Bay.

Match the Tile to Your Needs

Tile that will be used on a floor needs to be strong, tough, and resistant to scratches and stains. If the tile will be used on a wall—particularly for bathroom wainscot or a kitchen backsplash—a more important consideration than durability is how easy it is to clean. Dirt and grease are removed far more easily from smoothly glazed tiles than from unglazed tiles with textured surfaces or from porous stone tiles. But what if you're thinking about tile for a kitchen countertop, where both durability and ease of cleaning are important?

▲ A PRACTICAL PORCELAIN-TILE FLOOR laid in a random pattern reflects this laundry room's utilitarian roots. Tumbled natural slate on the countertops and on the decorative border above the sink reinforce this remodeled ranch home's new, rustic Southwestern décor.

◀ ▼ ALTHOUGH THE IRREGULAR SURFACE OF THESE HANDMADE TILES can make cleanup more challenging, the tiles give this countertop a rustic texture that matches well with the rough-sawn ceiling and cabinetry in the kitchen of this slope-side vacation home.

There are a number of industry-wide (but not universally applied) rating systems that grade tile for manufacturing quality, abrasion-resistance, hardness, and slipperiness. Fortunately, most manufacturers simplify the selection process by sticking with a widely used Class I (light-duty) to Class V (heavy-duty) rating system. In most cases, this information will be clearly marked on individual display tiles, but it should also be available in supporting literature from the manufacturer (see the sidebar on the facing page).

Most industry professionals will tell you that the best way to determine if a particular tile is right for your situation is to bring home samples and put them through their paces. To find out if a particular tile will be

▲ A FIREPROOF, EASILY CLEANED SURFACE that reflects heat back into the room, this white-tiled surround also reflects the neutral palette of the home's bright interior and showcases the woodstove's fire-engine red finish.

tough enough to be used as a flooring material in your home, try scuffing and scratching it with your favorite high heels or hiking boots; see what kinds of marks (if any) show up, and then see how easy those marks are to clean up. If you're interested in using a particular tile for a countertop, set a sample or two on top of your existing countertop and see how they stand up to the kind of wear and tear normally experienced in your kitchen.

Tough Enough?

SOME TILE MANUFACTURERS use the Mohs hardness scale, which was developed by geologists, to indicate how resistant a surface is to scratching. The scale ranges from 1 (the softest) to 10 (the hardest), and a medium-duty tile might earn a 5 or 6 Mohs rating. But you're more likely to encounter the ISO (International Standards Association) rating system, which is widely used by manufacturers to rate tiles for their resistance to abrasion. Here are the five categories:

- Class I: Suitable for walls only.
- Class II: For very light-duty floor use, such as in a second-floor bathroom.
- Class III: For medium-duty residential use, such as in a bathroom or kitchen.
- Class IV: For heavy-duty residential use, such as in entryways or high-traffic kitchens.
- Class V: For commercial use (but can be used residentially).

Tile Options

Evaluating the wide range of ceramic, stone, and other types of tile is easier when you first determine where and how a tile will be used. A floor tile used in a high-traffic situation needs to be tough and should hide dirt and scratches, while a wall tile can be chosen more for its looks than for its durability. Here's a cross section of some basic tile types, with a look at their distinguishing characteristics.

A CERAMIC WALL TILE WITH BLUE CRACKLE GLAZE. A decorative, glass-like glaze gives this tile its beauty. But beauty is only skin-deep; scratch through the glaze and the body of the tile shows through, so these tiles should only be used on walls.

B COMMERCIAL CERAMIC WALL TILE. Relatively inexpensive, this type of all-purpose wall tile has a soft, gypsum-based body that makes it easy to cut. Standard-grade tile is characterized by its uniform size and color; each tile is virtually identical to others in a particular manufacturing run.

C *ROSA VERONA* TUMBLED MARBLE. Like porcelain, marble has color all the way through, so deep scratches don't expose a different color. But like all stones, marble is porous and must be periodically sealed to help prevent staining.

D HANDMADE GLAZED WALL TILE. Handmade tiles have an irregular shape that creates a rich texture, making them an ideal choice for Arts and Crafts–influenced designs. Expect to find a considerable amount of color variation in the glazing.

E HANDMADE SANDED FLOOR TILE. The addition of a small amount of sand to the glaze of this tile gives it a slip-resistant finish—an important addition when using smooth tiles for flooring because they can be extremely slippery.

F PORCELAIN FLOOR TILE. Denser than ordinary ceramic tile and impervious to moisture, porcelain tile is tough and stain-resistant, making it an excellent choice for high-traffic areas. Porcelain tile can be glazed or unglazed and can range in size from small mosaics (2 in. by 2 in. sq. or smaller) to large floor tiles measuring 16 in. by 16 in. or more.

G LIMESTONE TILE. Slightly less dense than marble, limestone is also quite porous and can stain fairly readily unless properly sealed. Stones like limestone can be "cleft," so they'll leave an irregular surface, but usually they are "gauged" (or cut) and polished to varying degrees of smoothness depending on the desired look.

H STONE LOOK-ALIKE CERAMIC TILE. To get the look of stone without stone's high price or maintenance issues, many manufacturers now offer glazed ceramic tile that looks just like stone. Color variations within the glaze hide dirt between cleanings.

I MARBLE FLOOR OR WALL TILE. Depending on the degree of polishing applied to a stone tile like marble, it can be suitable for use on floors, walls, or both. Highly polished surfaces on a stone tile reflect light and brighten dark areas but show scratches and require more cleaning. Honed or matte finishes are better on floors because they're more slip-resistant and hide scratches better.

Take Stock of Your Lifestyle

Another factor to consider when choosing a particular type of tile is how much maintenance you'll be willing to devote to it in addition to the daily clean-up detail. Some tiles are virtually impervious to moisture, while others are relatively porous and can stain. For example, all stone tiles require periodic sealing to protect them from staining, as do low-fired unglazed pavers, such as Italian terra cotta or Mexican Saltillo tiles. Glazed ceramic tile, mosaics, and porcelain tile generally don't stain, so they don't need to be sealed (although the grout may need to be from time to time).

Whether the shine comes from a glaze or the highly polished surface of a stone tile, high-gloss tiles show scratches more readily than tiles with a matte finish. Some scratches on stone tile can be repaired by additional polishing, but on harder stones like granite, those scratches—though more difficult to put there in the first place—are tougher to remove.

Many less-expensive glazed wall tiles have a relatively soft, gypsum-based body, so if the hard glaze finish gets a deep scratch, the clay body will show through. However, a damaging scratch is less likely to occur if the tile is used solely for its designated purpose—to spruce up a wall.

In addition, some tiles simply show dirt more readily than others. If your family includes kids and pets, a tile with a durable, low-maintenance surface—such as a porcelain tile—with a finish rich in color variations will simplify your life considerably. All that it will require is periodic vacuuming and a quick mop once in a while. Save the marble for the master bath.

▲ HAND-PAINTED IN COLORS AND PATTERNS typical of eighteenth-century Portugal, these exquisite reproduction tiles create a refined, antique ambience that counterbalances the earthy terra cotta floor tile and contributes to the home's relaxed Mediterranean style.

Budget Tips and Tricks

Almost as astonishing as the wide range of tile choices is the wide range of tile prices that you'll encounter. Prices can dip below $2 per square foot for standard, white-glazed wall tiles, but expect basic floor tiles to cost from $2 to $5 or more per square foot. And if you've got your eye on something a little more exotic, like glass tile or a custom mosaic, prices escalate quickly—as much as $60 or more per square foot. And remember that these prices are for the tile only; installation costs vary depending on the region and the type of installation, but a rough guide is about $4 to $6 per square foot in addition to the cost of the tile.

Fortunately, there are a couple of strategies for managing costs. One is to allocate your tile dollars effectively. Expensive hand-made tiles and inexpensive factory-run tiles can be mixed and matched to good effect; save the high-priced tiles for borders or accents, where they'll really have a visual impact. Another strategy is to sleuth for seconds or discontinued tiles; many tile showrooms have "bargain basements" where these types of tiles, ordering mistakes, and overstock can be found, sometimes at significant savings.

◄ AN EFFECTIVE WAY to make the most of your tile budget is to mix a few colorful—and more expensive—hand-painted tiles with economical machine-made tiles, as was done in this elegant but low-key bath.

◀ ▲ EVEN A LITTLE BIT OF TILE can have a significant visual impact. When this Brooklyn brownstone's kitchen was renovated, handmade Italian tiles with a crackled finish (see the detail photo) were chosen for the backsplash to pick up colors found in the granite countertop and maple cabinetry. They also help reflect light back into the room. Though it measures only a few square feet, the backsplash is one of this kitchen's primary focal points.

▶ AVAILABLE IN A WIDE RANGE of colors, styles, and textures, stone and ceramic tiles are both challenging and richly rewarding design elements. Here, the tiled backsplash draws attention to the cook-top and range hood, while the more muted floor tile plays an understated role in the kitchen's design.

DESIGNING WITH TILE

Tile isn't as easily changed as paint, wall-paper, or carpet, which can be intimidating. But while it pays to be cautious, a more common mistake is to be overly so, result-ing in bland installations that don't really take advantage of the decorative possibili-ties that tile has to offer. You may want to rely on the expertise of a professional interior designer or at least adopt the tools and methods of the trade as you consider not only the physical characteristics of various tiles but also how standard elements of design—such as size, color, pattern, and texture—can be utilized to enhance the overall look of your project.

A detailed sketch is a good first step. In new construction, you may be able to rely on blueprints as you plan your design. If you're working with an existing space, you'll want to get out a tape measure and take accurate dimensions, jotting them down on graph paper to help you scale the installa-tion. Include the location and dimensions of existing fixtures, as well as an elevation sketch for vertical elements, such as a back-splash. These sketches will help you select appropriately sized and shaped tiles, decide on colors and textures, and plan a pattern.

Size and Shape

The scale of your project will help you determine the size (or sizes) of tile that will work the best. For example, an expansive floor generally looks better with large tiles, evidenced by the fact that most floor tiles are 12 in. by 12 in. or larger. However, small mosaic tiles historically have been used to make stunning floors, particularly in exceptionally large rooms. Limited spaces typically look better with smaller tiles because bulky tiles and bold patterns can overwhelm a small room or area.

Mixing several different sizes of the same type of tile is a particularly effective design tool. Keep in mind, though, that there can be a significant difference between the *nominal* and *actual* size of a tile, which can become a significant factor when mixing tiles from different manufacturers. For example, one manufacturer's nominal 4-in.-sq. tile may actually measure 3¾ in. sq., while another's may measure 4¼ in. sq., differences that aren't easily accommodated.

▲ THE FLOOR AND WALLS of this bathroom were tiled with small glass mosaics, making texture rather than pattern the primary design element. The deep color creates a sense of coziness in the space that balances the tiles' potentially cold effect.

About Grout

NO DISCUSSION ABOUT TILE would be complete without a look at grout, the material used to fill in the gaps between tiles. There are two broad categories: cement based and epoxy. Traditional cement-based grouts can be either sanded or unsanded; sanded grouts are used in joints ⅛-in. to ½-in. wide, while unsanded grouts are used in joints narrower than ⅛-in. (omit the sand in a wide joint and the grout is more likely to crack). Cement-based grouts may be modified with latex or polymer additives, which give the grout joint increased flexibility and improved stain resistance.

These grouts should be sealed to help protect them against staining and mildew.

Epoxy grout is virtually impervious to stains and mildew, making it an ideal choice for kitchen countertops and shower stalls. It's available in a wide range of colors, doesn't fade, doesn't need sealing, is easy to keep clean, and will last as long as the tile itself. A two-part mixture made up of resins and a coloring agent, epoxy grout also has some downsides. It's about four times as expensive as a modified cement-based grout, is considerably more demanding to work with, and can't be used with most stone and other porous tiles.

Knowing your project's exact dimensions will help you choose a tile size that harmonizes with your room's dimensions and best creates a pleasing pattern. Generally speaking, a tile installation looks best (and will require less labor and thus less money to install) when it's planned so that the fewest number of tiles need to be cut. For example, if you're installing an 8-in.-wide trim on a fireplace surround, choose 2-in.-, 4-in.-, or 8-in.-wide tiles rather than 3-in.-or 6-in.-wide tiles. If you're tiling a narrow hallway, avoid using large tiles laid on the diagonal, which results in very few "field"(uncut) tiles, requiring a lot of cutting and substantial waste.

In addition to size, tile shapes can be used to create interesting borders and other patterns. Shapes range from every geometric pattern imaginable to more organic shapes custom-made to suit your unique vision.

▲ A GOOD RULE OF THUMB: Choose large tiles for large areas. Here, terra cotta floor tiles finished with a stain of colored beeswax help this New Mexico house capture the warmth and atmosphere of traditional Southwest architecture.

▶ ANOTHER RULE OF THUMB: Be prepared to break the rules when using tile. Small glass mosaics in a blend of neutral shades create a uniquely textured surface on the floor of this contemporary kitchen.

Texture

There's a big difference in texture between the highly polished surface of a smoothly glazed tile and the rougher, irregular surface of an unglazed tile. Smooth or highly polished surfaces suggest more formal and dramatic spaces, and because they reflect light, they can help brighten areas that are dark and make colors more vivid.

Matte or textured finishes absorb light and give a tile more depth and can be used to create an intimate, informal look. Another advantage to richly textured tiles is that they hide dirt and fingerprints much better than a smooth tile, though they can also be a bit harder to clean.

▲ DECIDEDLY INFORMAL, this home's casual atmosphere and roughly textured, log-and-fieldstone walls are perfectly complemented by the earthy finish and irregular surface of handmade Mexican floor tiles. Although the tiles are unglazed, they are finished with a sealer that protects them from staining, helps brighten the room, and makes the floor easy to keep clean.

▶ HIGHLY POLISHED FINISHES suggest a more formal look, which is perfectly captured by these granite tiles as they gather light and create a dramatic "reflecting pool" on the floor of this paneled sitting room.

▶ WAVES OF LIGHT- AND DARK-BLUE, hand-chopped glass mosaic pieces—or tesserae—stand out against an almost pixilated background of green and blue glass tiles. Producing the same pattern in a different color palette—natural stone hues, for example— would give the design a more serenely elegant feel.

Color

Color is, of course, a matter of personal preference, but because of tile's permanence once installed, it's wise to temper your enthusiasm for a given color with a well-advised understanding of how color works in a room. Generally speaking, light or neutral colors make a space feel larger, while darker colors make a room feel smaller. Also, keep in mind that to many people, warm colors at the red end of the spectrum feel cozier and more intimate than those at the cooler blue end of the spectrum.

Remember, too, that light has a big impact on how color is perceived. Tile looks different in daylight than in artificial light, and different artificial light sources— fluorescent or halogen lighting, for instance— also affect how color is perceived. Not only that, but showroom catalogs don't always represent color accurately, and actual tile colors can vary slightly from production run to production run. Further complicating matters, the perception of color is altered by the presence of other colors, and small color samples—an individual tile, for instance— can't convey the effect of a block of color as accurately as larger samples.

To make sure that tile will look the way you expect it to, obtain samples and bring them home to view them in both daylight and artificial light before you install them. And if color uniformity from tile to tile is important, make sure that you purchase tiles from the same production run (this can be done by comparing lot numbers on each box).

Before deciding on a color scheme, do your homework. If the tile pattern is intricate with many colors, do a trial layout first, arranging and rearranging the tile until you're satisfied with the design. Or render the design with paint to see how all of the colors and patterns look together. On a practical note, keep in mind that, in general, lighter-colored tiles are more difficult to keep clean than darker tiles.

◀ COLOR TAKES CENTER STAGE in this Southwest-flavored kitchen, where the owners (who are also ceramic artists) created brightly hued tiles using custom-mixed glazes and plaster molds to match their collection of Depression-era tableware.

▲ AN ANTIQUE AND REFITTED GAS STOVE framed by a hearth-like enclosure, a vintage enameled cast-iron sink, and the generous use of classic white, 3-in. by 6-in. subway tiles create a light and bright kitchen with a 1920s ambience.

◀ IN A SWIRLING SALUTE to this renovated Mexican home's traditional adobe construction, ochre-colored stones collected from a dry riverbed and broken shards of black slate found in the neighboring mountains pave the central courtyard with pattern and color.

Pattern

Tile imposes a rigidly geometric pattern on a surface, which should be considered along with other design elements. Many people are satisfied with the pleasing orderliness of a straightforward grid-style installation, while others choose less-orthodox patterns to achieve varying looks.

Different patterns can be chosen to minimize or emphasize a room's characteristics. For example, vertical lines tend to emphasize height, so a pattern with a strong vertical component on a wall will make a room feel taller. Horizontal lines—in a chair-rail-type border, for instance—draw the eye outward, making a small room feel larger. Even relatively simple borders and small accents can have strong visual effects.

Because they're somewhat surprising, diagonal lines—tiles laid in a diamond pattern, for example—are dramatic. They can be used to give a space variety, movement, and excitement. Tile that is laid diagonally on a floor helps to visually expand the space, particularly if a room is long and narrow.

▶ VARIATIONS IN THE TILES' SCALE AND TEXTURE keep this bright white kitchen from being too stark and predictable. Twelve-inch-square floor tiles scale down to 6 in. sq. on the backsplash and 4 in. sq. on the countertop, while contrasting inserts add interest. The diagonal layout is a nice complement to the room's shape.

▲ THE HEXAGONAL GRID made by these classic mosaic floor tiles creates a busy pattern with lots of energy. The modified Greek key border with its straightforward grid helps temper the main floor, while the green tiles break up the expanse of white.

▲ PATTERN AND TEXTURE are two important factors to consider when designing with tile. The horizontal accent tiles add appeal and help visually expand this small shower, while the softer texture of the pillowed field tiles creates a more relaxed, informal feel than high-gloss tiles would.

Does Tile Absorb Water?

YES AND NO. The terms *vitreous* and *nonvitreous* indicate a tile's density and porosity, or its ability to absorb moisture. Vitreous tiles absorb very little moisture (less than 3%), making them suitable for use on floors as well as in wet or frost-prone areas. Nonvitreous tiles shouldn't be used in wet or exterior locations because they are highly absorbent. Most are rated in one of the following four categories by their manufacturers, but for a quick check, put a few drops of water on the back of the tile. If the water isn't absorbed, the tile is vitreous; if the water soaks in, the tile is nonvitreous.

- Nonvitreous: Easily absorbs water; unsuitable for outdoor use or in wet locations. Absorption rate of 7% +.
- Semivitreous: Limited outdoor use but generally suitable for most indoor applications. Absorption rates of 3% to 7%.
- Vitreous: Suitable for most exterior and wet applications. Absorption rates of 0.5% to 3%.
- Impervious: Dense, stain-resistant, and suitable for installation indoors and out. Less than 0.5% absorption rate.

2

Kitchens

I n most households, the kitchen is the home's focal point, the stage where the little dramas of daily life get played out. Here is where we prepare our meals, of course, but also where we have some of our most important conversations—with our spouse over a cup of coffee or with our kids during an afternoon snack or with our friends over an after-dinner drink. The kitchen is where pets pester us for table scraps, where bills get paid, and where homework gets done.

Because so much happens in the kitchen, it makes sense to choose surfaces and finishes that not only wear well and are easy to clean but that look terrific, too. Tile fits the bill perfectly. For instance, there's no other floor finish that offers the durability of tile; it can stand up to heavy foot traffic without wearing out, easily withstand all sorts of spills, and shrug off dirt with just a quick mopping.

Tile can be a great choice for countertops and backsplashes as well because of its heat and moisture resistance, while stove alcoves are a perfect venue for exploring tile's decorative possibilities. Simple or spectacular, traditional or contemporary, there's no limit to the possibilities for using one—or more—of the many different varieties of tile in the kitchen.

◄ AN ECLECTIC BLEND OF RUSTIC AND REFINED, this country kitchen features a tough floor of handmade stoneware tile with a glazed finish that ranges from green to red. A popular choice in traditional kitchens, the Delft-style wall tile design originated in Holland over 400 years ago.

Floors and Walls

THE FIRST STEP IN SELECTING just the right tile for your kitchen's floors and walls is to take stock of your lifestyle. Active families with children and pets would be well advised to place a high priority on practicality, choosing neutral and textured tiles that hide dirt well and clean up easily. If the kitchen has an entrance directly to the outdoors, extra durability may be a key issue; at the very least, floor tiles should be rated for medium- to heavy-use floors. And because kitchen floors are subject to splashing water and greasy spills, make sure floor tiles have an effective nonslip surface. You'll have more options with wall tiles because resilience isn't as much of an issue. Walls provide the perfect canvas to really explore the decorative possibilities of ceramic, stone, glass, and metal tile. And because most kitchen wall space is occupied by cabinets or appliances, you won't need large quantities of expensive tile to make a dramatic statement.

◄ RECLAIMED, ANTIQUE TERRA COTTA FLOOR TILES that have been cleaned and acid washed give this kitchen the flavor of Tuscany, which is further enhanced by the handcrafted tiles used on the countertop, backsplash, and range hood.

◀ WHEN THE KITCHEN of this 1950s Federal revival-style house was renovated, the backsplash was dressed up with 2-in.-sq. tiles made of tumbled stone and set on the diagonal. A few decorative ceramic tiles and a geometric border of stone mosaics provide contrast and pick up colors found in the kitchen's woodwork.

▶ THE *RAKU*-FIRED TILES on this kitchen's walls and countertops have an almost iridescent crackled surface with surprising color variations, creating a richly organic contrast to the cooler palette of the natural limestone, 12-in. by 12-in. floor tiles, and stainless steel stove and range hood.

▲ **THOUGH THE OPEN FLOOR PLAN IS CONTEMPORARY,** this kitchen's terra cotta floor and soaring arches help to give it an Old World look. Tile detailing—on the backsplash, around the window, and inside one of the arches—contributes an elegant yet comfortable touch.

◀ ▲ NARROW, GALLEY-STYLE KITCHENS naturally have focused traffic patterns that can wear out a floor quickly. This one is located on an island in Maine's Casco Bay, so sand and grit compound the problem, making tile a logical choice for the floor. Besides the tile's bold pattern and color, which add some zest to the kitchen's white palette, the strong diagonal pattern helps to visually widen the space and expands seamlessly into the informal dining nook at the far end of the kitchen.

Designing Tile Patterns to Best Advantage

A GALLEY-STYLE KITCHEN is an efficient design because it places most appliances and work centers within just a few steps of one another. But in this type of kitchen (and in other rooms that are long and narrow), a tile floor that's installed in a straight pattern creates prominent grout lines that emphasize the room's length and make the room feel even narrower (drawing at right).

One way to minimize this effect is to use smaller tiles, which tends to de-emphasize the grout lines. But an even better strategy is to lay the tile diagonally, which tends to draw the eye toward the sides of a room, making it feel wider (drawing at far right).

Straight grid   Diagonal grid

Floor tile installed in a straight pattern makes a narrow room feel narrower (left), while tile installed diagonally helps a narrow room feel wider (right).

◄ ▼ TILE CAN BE USED IN COMBINATION with other materials in unexpected ways. Here, oak planks inlaid into the floor divide up the diagonally laid tile of this multitasking room creating an interesting grid pattern.

► WITH A DIRECT CONNECTION TO THE OUTDOORS, the country kitchen in this converted, stone Pennsylvania schoolhouse needs the rugged durability of its tile floor. The tile's classic black-and-white pattern creates a surprisingly formal contrast to the room's relaxed style.

▲ WHEN THIS SUBURBAN RANCH HOUSE was remodeled, walls were removed to open up the floor plan and the ceiling was raised to add more light. But the kitchen's tiled floor helps differentiate it from the adjoining living area; the reinterpretation of the classic black-and-white tile pattern gives the space vibrancy.

▶ GENERALLY BUILT OUT OF STRAIGHTFORWARD MATERIALS and with a simple design, walk-in pantries offer a lot of storage bang for the buck. An appropriate flooring choice, the large, commercial-grade porcelain tiles used here are economical, hold up well under foot, and clean up easily with a damp mop.

◀ ▲ INTRICATELY PATTERNED WALL TILES from the Xabregas region of Portugal inject color and drama into this otherwise stark white kitchen. The natural, intertwining shapes hand-painted in blue and gold are examples of the strong Moorish influence often found in historic and contemporary Spanish and Portuguese tile designs.

◄ WHEN CHOOSING WALL TILE FOR A KITCHEN, consider the amount of available natural and artificial lighting and the amount of wall area that isn't covered by shelves, appliances, or cabinetry. Remember that darker colors tend to absorb light and require more illumination, but they can also make very large spaces feel more intimate.

Living with Tile

LIKE ANY HARD SURFACE, tile can be uncomfortable to stand on for long periods of time. It can also be cold under foot—a good feature in hot climates but not so desirable in cold climates. To make your tile floor more comfortable, consider adding cushioned area rugs in front of the kitchen sink and other often-used work areas. And an in-floor radiant heating system will turn a cold tile floor into a room-size radiator that provides silent, even heat right where it's needed most. You'll be walking around barefoot even on the coldest January days.

◄ CLASSIC WHITE TILES ARE A POPULAR CHOICE in both contemporary and period kitchens, and can be used to create spaces that look clean and bright. These subway tiles, popular during the 1920s and 1930s, are a good match for this kitchen's vintage look.

What's Raku?

WHILE MOST TILE MAKERS STRIVE FOR uniformity in their glazes, those that practice the traditional Japanese process of *raku* seek just the opposite.

In this process, tile is glazed and fired in a kiln, then dipped into various materials, including wood shavings, sawdust, or straw. They ignite on the tile's surface, chemically interact with the glaze, and leave behind a film of ash and carbon. The magic is revealed when the cooled and blackened tiles are cleaned off: each one has a unique combination of iridescent colors, swirling smoke patterns, and crackled surfaces.

▼ ► FRENCH LIMESTONE FLOOR TILES and pale-yellow handmade wall tiles provide a light counterpoint to the dark oak cabinetry, black granite countertop, and stainless steel appliances in the kitchen of this renovated Shingle-style house. The delicate patterns on the tile and matching molding (see detail) were produced by directly imprinting the wet clay with actual leaves before kiln-firing.

▲ IN A DESIGN INSPIRED BY THE VILLAGE FOUNTAINS found throughout Italy, this farmhouse-style sink features a high-arched backsplash composed of custom terra cotta tiles framing a latticework ladder of diagonally set, bone-colored, glazed tiles divided by tiny travertine mosaics.

Countertops

COUNTERTOPS TILED WITH CERAMIC OR STONE aren't for everybody. Tiled countertops have a hard, uneven surface that's unforgiving to knives, glassware, and fine china. But tile is also sanitary, tough, and moisture- and heat-resistant, and it offers design possibilities that just can't be matched with any other countertop material. Best of all, tile is extremely versatile. It can be used selectively—around sinks and stoves, for example, where its practical qualities can be put to best use—and matched easily with other countertop materials. Or it can be used exclusively to create a one-of-a-kind countertop that uniquely enhances the rest of your kitchen.

▲ MORE APPROPRIATE THAN A STONE SLAB in this bungalow-styled kitchen, the countertop is composed of machine-made tiles with a uniform matte glaze, which delicately contrast with the handcrafted backsplash field tiles. Decorative accent tiles in the style of Batchelder (a prominent tile maker in the 1930s) offer textural contrast and are an appropriate match for the Arts and Crafts–influenced oak cabinetry.

◀ THE COUNTERTOP'S HANDMADE TILE has an uneven surface that adds subtle texture to this monochromatic kitchen. Wisely, most of the cutting and food prep takes place on the butcher-block counter of the kitchen island, a surface that is more knife-friendly.

△ GLOSSY GREEN, GLAZED CERAMIC TILES on this kitchen island countertop provide a colorful contrast to the kitchen's white painted cabinetry, create a reflective surface that helps enhance the room's natural light, and hint at the colors found in the landscape outside.

Cost-Effective Stone Countertops

Like the look of a stone-slab countertop but not the price? Consider using stone tile instead. Many different types of stone— including granite and marble—are available in economically priced, 3/8-in.-thick by 12-in.-sq. tiles. When installed with tight grout joints, these tiles offer the look of a slab for less than half the cost.

You won't be able to install an under-mount sink with these tiles, and because they have a thinner edge than a typical 1¼-in.-thick slab of stone, they'll require a different edge treatment. But considering that solid-slab countertops can run more than $125 per sq. ft., stone tiles can be a bargain.

△ LOCATED AT AN ELEVATION OF 7,000 FT. near Taos, New Mexico, this adobe-style house features a passive solar design, adobe walls for thermal storage, and finishes —including cabinets of cherry and alder and a countertop of highly variegated 6-in. by 6-in. ceramic tile—that emphasize the natural colors and textures found in the surrounding landscape.

► THERE ARE VARIOUS WAYS to finish the edge of a tile countertop, and most manufacturers offer a variety of trim tiles for that purpose. But these handmade tiles are trimmed at both the counter edge and at the top of the backsplash with a simple cherry wood bullnose to match the kitchen's cabinetry.

► THIS KITCHEN WAS ORIGI-NALLY DESIGNED to accommodate a farmhouse-style sink, which has a front apron that extends down over the sink cabinet. Instead, a panel of 2-in. by 2-in. slate tiles, which match the slate-tiled countertop, was used to fill the opening in the custom-made maple cabinetry.

▲ ▼ THE EXTRA-THICK, HANDMADE TILES used on this island countertop's perimeter match the thickness of the dark soapstone work surface and provide a substantial finished edge to the countertop. An artist working in clay can create custom designs to each customer's specifications and re-create them in tile using plaster of Paris molds.

Stains and Sealers

Like many other common foods and products found in a kitchen, red wine is acidic and can stain many types of stone tiles. In addition, many cleaners also contain mild acids and will actually dull some ceramic tiles, as well as polished marble and limestone.

To protect your tile countertop, be sure to use appropriate sealers that are regularly applied as recommended by the manufacturer. Also, keep in mind that regular sanded or unsanded grout will stain too and will also need to be sealed.

What You Should Know about Tile Countertops

ALMOST ANY TILE can be used for a countertop…as long as you understand its limitations. For example, some dark and glossy tiles scratch relatively easily and show those scratches readily. Softer stones—such as limestone—also scratch easily, though those scratches can theoretically be sanded out. In general, highly polished ceramic and stone surfaces—even granite—tend to show scratches, while matte finishes do a better job of hiding them. Does this mean that these types of tile can't be used? No, but you'll need to plan on using cutting boards and protecting the tile from pots and pans.

Handmade tiles can also be used to create terrific-looking countertops. But keep in mind that these types of tile are irregularly sized and require wider grout joints than production tile to accommodate the variations in their size and uneven edges. When combined with their generally rougher surface texture, this can result in countertop surfaces that are fairly uneven. Also, consider using an epoxy grout for your countertop (though epoxy grouts can't be used with some stones) because it is easier to maintain and won't stain like a sanded grout.

▲ HANDMADE TILE HAS UNEVEN EDGES AND AN IRREGULAR SURFACE, and it needs to be installed with fairly wide grout joints, making it somewhat hazardous for tippy objects such as vases and wine glasses.

◄ TILE COUNTERTOPS ARE HEAT-RESISTANT AND EASY TO CLEAN and work well with drop-in-style sinks (as shown). Be sure to use cutting boards when working on a tile countertop, which will protect both the tile and the edges of your knives.

◄ SET IN A DIAGONAL ORIENTATION with wide grout lines that emphasize their pattern, the handcrafted tiles on this kitchen countertop have a textural quality that matches the rustic wood surfaces of the log home and a neutral color that enhances the room's natural light.

◄ ▲ THOUGH THE SINK AND COUNTER-TOP ARE NEW (see photo left), the exuberant green-and-yellow tiles were carefully chosen to match the existing tile work of this vintage 1930s Los Angeles kitchen (above). They are typical of the art deco-influenced Spanish Revival character of other homes in the surrounding historic neighborhood.

Backsplashes

THOUGH OCCUPYING only a few square feet, the wall space between countertops and upper cabinetry is prime kitchen real estate. Located just below eye level and highly visible throughout the kitchen—and sometimes other living spaces—a well-conceived tile backsplash can have a decorative effect that far outweighs the effort and expense of installing it. The backsplash can be simple: a single or double row of tiles that matches the countertop and extends along its length. Or for greater visual impact (and easier cleaning), the backsplash can extend all the way to the bottom edge of the upper cabinetry, completely covering the exposed wall. In either case, the backsplash is the place where custom-made or hand-painted tiles, murals, and other kinds of decorative tilework—which would be too delicate and/or costly to use elsewhere in the kitchen—can be used to great artistic effect.

▼ GLASS TILES IN SHADES OF BEIGE with hints of silver, gold, and copper seem to be illuminated from behind in this mosaic bar-sink backsplash. Recessed lights in the overhead cabinets are the true source of illumination, illustrating the way in which lighting can enhance the effect of a tile installation.

▲ BECAUSE A LOT OF TIME is spent at the kitchen sink, it's a logical place to use decorative tiles. These designs were hand-painted onto widely available bisque tiles using a variety of glazes, then kiln-fired to produce permanent works of art.

▲ LIKE A COMFORTABLE QUILT, this backsplash's rich texture invites both the eye and the hand and adds subtle blue and caramel colors to a house built largely with natural materials. Slight variations in the colors and sizes of the handcrafted tiles add to the composition's charm.

▲ CHOSEN TO REFLECT the home's "rustic contemporary" theme, this backsplash of richly glazed field tiles, along with a matching decorative band of accent tiles that's highlighted with steel and bronze trim, helps create a balance between the warm wood of the cabinetry and the cool stainless steel appliances.

◄ HANDMADE TILES GLAZED IN EARTH TONES add a subtle note of color to the natural hues of stone and oak in this Craftsman-influenced kitchen.

▼ ▶ RENOVATED ON A SHOESTRING BUDGET around an original Youngstown metal sink/cabinet, much of this 1930s-style kitchen's color comes from the Depression-era china displayed on open shelving, which inspired the backsplash of 18 handmade tiles. The tiles were press-molded with Southwestern scenes and custom-glazed to match.

▼ COMPOSED OF GLASS MOSAIC TILES, the backsplash in this Shaker-inspired kitchen contrasts nicely with the yellow pine flooring and fir cabinetry's warm wood tones and muted simplicity, as well as with the neutral limestone countertop.

Designing a Tile Backsplash

REGARDLESS OF WHAT **surfacing material has been used for your kitchen countertops, tile** offers a perfect medium for making a splash with your backsplash. But before diving into the design, think about how your countertop is used. If yours is the kind that gets cluttered with appliances and accessories, it probably makes little sense spending a lot of time and money on a design that is barely visible. Instead, plan a plain yet functional backsplash, and save your decorating dollars for another location with more visual impact. Also, zero in on your kitchen's focal points—probably above the sink and stove—and emphasize these areas in your overall backsplash design.

Your backsplash layout can start out as a simple sketch, but it's also important to note and measure important physical characteristics that may have an impact on your design, such as the location of wall outlets, windows, and upper cabinetry. These can be drawn on a sheet of graph paper, along with your cabinet layout. Remember that tile represents a relatively inflexible grid, so graph paper is a perfect medium for planning your design, as long as you measure accurately and draw everything to scale. This will help you select tile that requires a minimum of cutting, which will result in a better-looking (and less-expensive) installation.

Graph paper is an excellent choice for sketching out potential tile designs. First, accurately measure and record cabinetry dimensions and the location of windows, fixtures, and other features. Then use graph paper to plan your layout, experimenting with patterns, colors, and tile sizes to achieve the look you want.

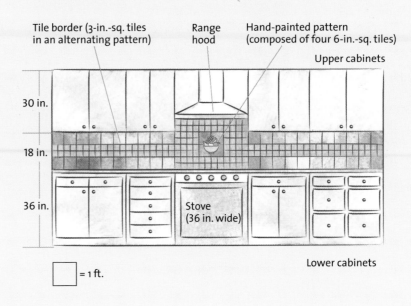

Tile border (3-in.-sq. tiles in an alternating pattern) — Range hood — Hand-painted pattern (composed of four 6-in.-sq. tiles)

Upper cabinets

30 in.
18 in.
36 in.

Stove (36 in. wide)

☐ = 1 ft.

Lower cabinets

Tile Backsplash Is Key to a Kitchen Makeover

WHEN THE OWNERS of this 1840s brick house decided to update the kitchen, it had sound cabinetry and a relatively new Corian™ countertop but dated appliances and a bland décor. Because they were on a budget, the homeowners decided to work within the existing floor plan, retaining the countertops and cabinetry while upgrading the appliances and wall finishes.

A key element in the makeover was a new tile backsplash of unglazed porcelain mosaic tiles; arranged in a brick-like pattern, the three different tile sizes give the wall color and texture and match the character of the house's exterior. They're sealed with a special sealer/color enhancer, which protects the tile and grout against grease and brings out the color and depth of the tiles.

And although they cost about $18 per sq. ft., the total project only required about 70 sq. ft. of tile. To provide a focal point and to break up the uniformity of the wall, a 1-ft.-sq. bronze medallion—actually a composite tile with an aged bronze finish—was added over the stove. At about $125 each, these specialty composite tiles aren't cheap, but they're easy to install and add a lot of visual impact. Total cost for the makeover, including new tile, paint, appliances, and labor: about $8,000.

▲ A FOCAL POINT IN THE KITCHEN, this 12-in.-sq. medallion is an example of new tile-making technology, where various types of metallic finishes—including the aged bronze shown here—can be applied to ceramic or composite tiles, creating a unique, decorative look.

◀ THE KEY INGREDIENT IN A MODESTLY PRICED KITCHEN MAKEOVER, this new backsplash features brick-like, unglazed porcelain mosaic tiles that give the walls a texture to match the character of the home's 1840 exterior.

▲ THOUGH EXPENSIVE, a little bit of glass tile can have a significant decorative effect. Here, the frosted glass tiles on the backsplash have the colors and texture of sea glass, a year-round reminder of summers spent on the beach with friends and family.

▲ OLD-FASHIONED, PARIS-STYLE SUBWAY TILES with a pillowed profile have a brick-like texture and contribute to the vintage feel of this cottage kitchen, part of a renovated 1860s Maine horse barn. The unusual window sash—with alternating clear and colored glass panes—was original to the old barn.

◀ A HAND-PAINTED (rather than glazed) mural of native Maine wildflowers on a field of plain white, machine-made tiles lends a delightful touch in this renovated coastal Maine cottage. The paint—called Pébéo Porcelaine 150™—can be applied to almost any glazed tile and baked in an oven to 300° F for a durable, permanent finish.

Cooking Alcoves and Range Hoods

I F YOU'RE A SERIOUS COOK, the surfaces adjacent to your stove can get a real workout. Sometimes it seems that splatters of hot grease and tomato sauce end up everywhere, so a protective finish that cleans up easily is almost as important as the stove itself. And because a stove usually breaks up a countertop as well as lower and upper cabinetry, it becomes a visual as well as a functional focal point in a kitchen. A beautifully tiled finish around a cooking alcove just makes perfect sense. And if you've installed a commercial-style stove in your kitchen that generates a lot of heat, you've almost certainly installed a high-capacity range hood as well, which provides yet another opportunity to incorporate unique tile designs.

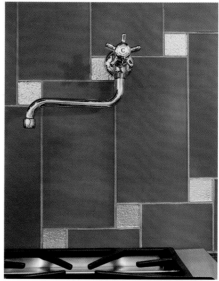

◄ ▲ CHOSEN FOR EASE OF CLEANING as well as good looks, these azure glass tiles have an etched rather than glossy finish; grease cleans easily off the surface without streaking or leaving an oily residue. Smaller silver glass tile accents (see detail photo) emphasize the range hood's geometry and pick up highlights from the Blue Pearl granite countertops and accent over the cooktop.

▶ DECORATIVE TILE MURALS—like this contemporary domestic vignette—that depict scenes from daily life have a long tradition that dates back to European and Mediterranean tin-glazed styles of the sixteenth and seventeenth centuries. Now they can be hand-painted, silk-screened, stenciled, or applied with decals.

◀ EXTENDING ALL THE WAY TO THE CEILING, the large, brick-like tiles on the range hood help balance this kitchen's spaciousness and call attention to the vibrantly colored, handcrafted Mexican tiles of the alcove, which suggest the saturated, rustic hues of the French countryside.

▼▶ DARK CHERRY CABINETRY and a backsplash of diagonally set *rosa verona* tumbled marble field tiles give this kitchen a rich look. Picture-framed by a ceramic tile border, the mural—along with the coordinating accents on the range hood—is silk-screened onto the tiles, which are then sealed with a durable protective coating after installation. At less than a quarter of the cost of comparable hand-painted tiles, silk-screened decorative tiles offer an economical alternative and are available in a wide range of styles, colors, and patterns.

◀ ALREADY DISTRESSED AND AGED by years of use, reclaimed, antique paver tiles that have been removed from the floors of old French farmhouses have a beautiful patina and are soft enough so that they can be easily shaped, as illustrated by the edge treatments of this kitchen's countertop and recessed alcove.

▶ AN EXAMPLE OF THE RESURGENT INTEREST in art tile from the early twentieth century, the stove alcove in this renovated 1912 house in Brookline, Mass., is composed of tile from Moravian Tile-works, a company that still uses its original 1930s mold designs to make hand-pressed and hand-painted tile.

▼ THE NEUTRAL TONES of this kitchen's white cabinetry and limestone countertops are energized by a grid-work pattern composed of lighter *botticino* and darker *verde* marble tiles on the backsplash and arched cooking alcove.

▲ THE TWIN MEDALLIONS, surrounded by a grid of cut tiles, and matching rope molding that decorate this cooking alcove are pressed out of a synthetic tile that has an aluminum facing. Closely matched stone tiles situated above, between, and below the composite tiles complete this striking installation.

A Quilted Tile Backsplash

THE COMMERCIAL-STYLE RANGES that are so popular today offer a perfect opportunity to take advantage of tile's practical qualities (tough and easy to clean) and decorative possibilities (as limitless as your imagination—and budget). Generally 6 in. to 18 in. wider than standard kitchen ranges, these big units require a lot of floor and wall space. They also put out a lot of heat and need to be exhausted by high-capacity range hoods; most offer a stainless steel backsplash that covers and protects the nearly 6 sq. ft. between the top of the range and the bottom of the range hood.

But some people, like Patricia Ryan Madson of El Granada, Calif., find all that metal to be too overwhelming. She loves quilting, and when she and her husband found these Spanish multicolored patchwork tiles, they knew they had found the answer to the bare drywall that sat above their stainless steel range for nearly two years after it had been installed. Pat and her husband, Ron, arranged and rearranged the 4-in. tiles, which are patterned after Indian fabric designs, into a pleasing mosaic, then picture-framed the design with green border tiles.

COLORFUL SPANISH TILE IS USED to make the heat- and splatter-proof quilt that hangs above this commercial-style range. Two fold-down warming racks are bolted to the wall above the range.

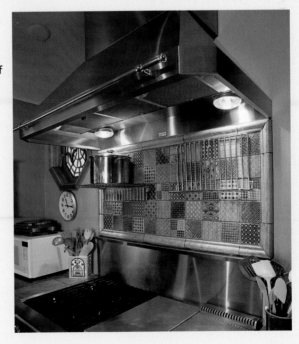

Finishing Touches

Because tile is such a versatile finish material, there are a number of places around the kitchen where it can be used to provide a final decorative touch. Walls are an obvious place to start. For example, consider adding either a full wainscot treatment or a simple, molding-tile chair rail, or embellishing a soffit with a few decorative tiles. Another possibility is to replace your wood baseboards with tile. Door and window casings also lend themselves to tile finishes. And if there's furniture in your kitchen—a dining table, a sideboard or dry sink, or a serving credenza, for example—tile can be used to dress it up. All of these ideas can be incorporated as part of an original decorative plan, or they can be added spontaneously as inspiration strikes…and the budget allows.

▶ A CURVED STANDING BAR creates both a buffer between the kitchen and the living and dining areas and a comfortable place to socialize in this updated 1938 Spanish bungalow. It's clad with 4-in.-sq. tiles of Indian slate and topped with a solid slab of granite to match the countertops.

◄ VERTICAL SLATE TILES that match this kitchen's slate backsplash curve gracefully around the kitchen island and are interspersed with smaller pewter medallion insets that echo the stainless steel finishes of the refrigerator and range hood. The effect is dramatic and stately.

▼ STOCK, BLACK-GLAZED CHERRY KITCHEN CABINETRY is dressed up with a custom-made marble mosaic, creating an elegant sideboard area that serves the dining room while still remaining functionally connected with the adjoining kitchen.

▲ COLLECTORS OF CONTEMPORARY ART, the owners of this kitchen turned to the colors found in a clock by one of their favorite artists for inspiration. They choose multi-hued glass tiles with both glossy and matte finishes for the backsplash, cooking alcove, and dining table of their vibrantly renovated kitchen.

3

Bathrooms

Of all the rooms in a house, none has changed quite so dramatically in both function and appearance over the past two decades as the bathroom. When bathrooms first moved into the house at the turn of the twentieth century, they were customized and built to last by craftsmen, with rugged, enameled cast-iron fixtures and durable—and often beautifully executed—tile finishes.

But with the introduction of mass-produced housing and plastics, bathrooms evolved into rather prosaic, box-shaped rooms filled with forgettable fixtures and nondescript finishes. Luckily, the pendulum has swung back now, and bathrooms have emerged from the proverbial—and literal—closet. They're bigger, bolder, more specialized, and more representative of the personalities of those who use them. That makes them, once again, perfect candidates for all of the creative possibilities that tile has to offer.

And tile offers practicality, as well as beauty; it can stand up to all the abuses bathroom materials take. When properly installed and maintained, stone, ceramic, and other types of tile will stand up to water and resist chemicals without providing sanctuary to mold, mildew, or bacteria. From floors and walls to custom showers and intimate bathing alcoves, tile can be used sparingly or exclusively; it's perfectly at home in any bathroom environment.

◀ ILLUSTRATING THE WIDE RANGE OF POSSIBILITIES that different sizes and types of tile bring to the design and construction of contemporary bathrooms, this exquisite California bathroom offers a Moorish influenced oasis amidst the hustle and bustle of urban Los Angeles living.

Floors and Walls

UNLIKE KITCHENS, MOST BATHROOMS aren't subject to heavy-duty foot traffic. With the exception of powder rooms and multi-purpose bathrooms located on the first floor, abrasion and scratch resistance is less of a factor than slip resistance, which is always important in the presence of moisture. For the best combination of traction underfoot and ease of cleaning, steer clear of smoothly glazed or highly polished tile, as well as tile with a gritty surface.

Bathroom floors are generally quite small and interrupted by fixtures. Bold or complicated tile designs are difficult to execute well in such a limited space, so simple field tiles—perhaps framed by a border—are a good choice for most bathroom floors. Bathroom walls are also relatively busy and punctuated with windows, mirrors, shower doors, and cabinets. An effective tile design will complement the bathroom's style and integrate all of the various interruptions into a logical and cohesive pattern.

▶ TRANSLUCENT, GREEN SEA-GLASS TILES and large-format, glazed ceramic floor tiles set on the diagonal help this relatively small bathroom feel larger. The glass tile mural above the tub creates a focal point that helps compensate for the room's lack of natural light.

◀ MULTIHUED MOSAIC TILES were used to add a splash of color-ful contrast to the more muted natural finishes in this narrow bathroom. They also unify the various surfaces in the room by bordering the large-format floor tiles, framing the mirror over the sink, and extending around the room like a chair rail above the ceramic tile wainscot.

▲ AN EXQUISITE TILE "BATH MAT" matches the colorful mosaic walls of this contemporary, Moorish-influenced bath. Tile rugs were tradi-tionally used in hot Mediterranean climates to add carpet-like patterns and colors to a room while keeping it cool and easy to maintain. Now many manufacturers offer lines of tile—complete with fringe—specifically intended for creating different styles of tile rugs.

◀ COMBINING OLD AND NEW ELEMENTS in a playful way, the glass-mosaic-tiled countertop in this spacious powder room floats against honed marble wall tiles. Stone gives the room a grounded and timeless quality, while the horizontal glass-tile accents emphasize the width of the room and suggest a chair rail, an impression reinforced by the diagonally laid tile below and the running bond pat-tern above.

▲ TAKING FULL ADVANTAGE of this toilet's unique, wall-mounted design, a tiny—though fully functional—basement half-bath features a rug-like, marble tile mosaic floor that helps brighten the space while picking up the warm tones of the wood-paneled wainscot.

▲ A WARM GREEN OASIS rather than a sterile white laboratory, this colorful bathroom features a mosaic tile "rug" that matches the framing around the mirror. Typical of handcrafted tiles, there's a range of color variation in the field tiles used on the floor and walls, which adds further texture to the room.

▶ BLACK AND WHITE is a classic bathroom floor pattern that lends itself to a variety of interpretations. These unglazed, porcelain mosaic tiles have a flat, nonreflective finish, and they provide excellent traction, as well as showing no signs of wear even after years of use.

▲ DEMONSTRATING TILE'S RICH cultural connotations, this guest bathroom (in a historic Hollywood home) was given a fantasy Moroccan treatment with the help of a richly figured, ceramic tile floor and porcelain mosaic wall tiles embedded in *tadleck*, a traditional Moroccan plaster.

Cool Tile, Warm Floor

If there's a disadvantage to having a tiled bathroom floor, it's that it can feel cold, especially to bare feet. Fortunately, it's possible to install a thin-profile, electric radiant-heat mat underneath your tile floor that will warm it up to a cozy temperature.

There are now a variety of electric radiant systems on the market, but basically they all consist of a matrix of electric wires embedded in a thin fabric "blanket." Thermostatically controlled and thin enough so that they don't significantly affect the height of the finished floor, electric radiant-heat mats are available in standard and (more expensive) custom sizes and cost about as much to operate as a 100-watt light bulb. (See Resources on p. 152 for ordering information.)

▶ DARK ON WHITE—in this case, polished *verde* and *carrara* marble—is a classic decorating scheme that lends bold formality to a room. Polished marble can be slippery underfoot, but in this bathroom the smaller 6-in. by 6-in. tiles provide more grout lines, adding traction.

Slippery when Wet

ANY SMOOTH SURFACE **can become dangerously slick when it gets wet. So when choosing a tile for a shower floor, steer clear of smoothly glazed ceramic tiles and polished stones. A better choice is tile that has a rough or textured surface. Manufacturers refer to a tile's coefficient of friction (COF) to indicate how much traction it provides, and in many cases, they will include this information on tile rated for floor use. Look for a number higher than 0.60 to indicate adequate traction control, or ask your salesperson if this information is available.**

Another way to increase traction underfoot is to use smaller tiles with more grout lines, which helps to create a textured, nonskid surface. An added benefit of smaller tiles is that they conform more easily to the sloped surfaces found on the floor of a shower and are thus less likely to crack. These qualities help to explain the longtime popularity of unglazed, porcelain mosaic tiles for bathroom floors. Typically mounted on 12-in. by 12-in. or 12-in. by 24-in. sheets for easy installation, porcelain mosaics have a tough clay body that is stain proof and won't chip easily.

TILE WITH A SMOOTH SURFACE, such as glazed ceramic tile (top) and polished stone (bottom) become extremely slippery when they get wet and shouldn't be used for a shower floor. Smaller tiles with a textured surface (center) provide better traction and conform well to the shape of a shower floor as it slopes toward the drain.

◄ A SMALL DECORATIVE PATTERN introduced in the floor becomes a bold geometric border that draws a firm line around the top of this bathroom's beadboard wainscot. The pattern is simple and elegant but still adds design muscle to this otherwise neutral bath.

Details Make the Difference for a Period Look

IN A TILE SHOWROOM, **your eye might be drawn to dramatic glass or stone tiles that glimmer like jewels...and have a price to match. But the beauty of tile is found not just in individual pieces but also in the overall designs that can be created with a few relatively simple components. Designs that take advantage of accents and borders mixed with straightforward (and far less expensive) "field" tiles have a long tradition that you can draw on as you create a period feel for your own bath.

This Arts and Crafts-influenced bath remodel, for example, features a floor consisting of widely available 1-in. hexagonal mosaics and a geometrically patterned border made up of contrasting dark-green tiles. This particular pattern involves a lot of cutting (and thus more expense), but small mosaics lend themselves to a wide variety of other geometric designs as well. The walls feature 3-in. by 6-in. white subway-style tiles, which are economical, with more expensive accents that match the floor border. Besides giving this bathroom a classic look, the white tiles help brighten the room, while the details along the borders add visual interest and a display of appreciation for the work of a craftsman.

▲ A STRONG GEOMETRICAL PATTERN AT THE CORNERS and along the borders creates visual interest and illustrates the homeowners' appreciation for the craftsman's handiwork.

▶ THIS ARTS AND CRAFTS-INFLUENCED BATHROOM MAKEOVER features white hexagonal floor tile embellished with geometric detailing and subway wall tile accented with simple, contrasting trim to give the room a traditional look.

▲ OLD HOUSES OFTEN HAVE SAGGING FLOORS AND CROOKED WALLS, which can require creative tiling solutions. Here, a tapered threshold helps match the old sloping floor to the new (and level) tile floor.

▲ TURNED ON THE DIAGONAL, this checkerboard-patterned tile floor injects this traditional bathroom with a touch of drama. Running tiles on the diagonal is also a good technique for visually widening the space.

▲ DECORATIVE ACCENTS like this tumbled marble mosaic can be precut and premounted on numbered sheets, simplifying installation and making the mosaic more affordable. The surrounding floor tiles are travertine, a porous sedimentary stone riddled with small holes caused by escaping gases when the stone was formed.

► LARGE *VERDE* MARBLE TILES set closely together have minimal grout lines, which helps emphasize the stone's veined patterns, while blending in with the marble slab countertop and giving this bathroom a masculine, monolithic quality.

◄ ▲ WAINSCOT IS A TRADITIONAL BATHROOM ELEMENT that's given a new twist here with the use of silver-gray glass mosaic tiles. Glass tile is available in a range of surface finishes; these aren't perfectly flat and have irregular edges that give them a rough, shimmering texture, creating a sharp and interesting contrast to the smoothly polished marble floor tiles.

◄ ALL MADE OF GLASS, the tiles, sink, and countertop of this powder room combine to create iridescent color and a fragile beauty. An environmentally responsible choice, these glass mosaic tiles are made largely from recycled bottles that have been cleaned and crushed into a substance called "cullet."

Unify Your Bathroom Design with Tile

BATHROOMS ARE TYPICALLY SMALL, with walls that are interrupted by fixtures, windows, shower valves, and electrical switches and outlets. A good wall tile design can help unify all of these elements into a cohesive whole while creating sight lines that enhance the room's feeling of spaciousness. The key is in locating and aligning in as logical a manner as possible all of the various items that interrupt the wall plane, and then linking them together with your tile design.

For example, the top of the sink—roughly from 30 in. to 36 in. above the floor—can establish the starting point for a strong horizontal line. If there is a window in the bathroom, its sill can be set close to this line. This is also a good height to set the shower control, even though it may be located on an adjacent wall. This horizontal alignment need not be exact; remember that the backsplash design (as well as the size of the tile used to build the backsplash) can be varied to make up any differences in the relative elevations of these components.

Because tile creates vertical, as well as horizontal, sight lines, vertical alignment is also important. Minor variations from the vertical line—a showerhead or spout that is off-center from a control, for example—are emphasized by tile's vertical grout lines. Thus, it's important to plan your fixture layout so that variations from logical vertical or horizontal arrangements look intentional.

TILE ALIGNMENT

Tile can be used to unify a bathroom design, but it helps if other elements—fixtures, controls, and windows and doors, for example—are oriented logically with one another. A strong horizontal line, such as a backsplash that extends out around all four walls, helps to make a small room feel larger.

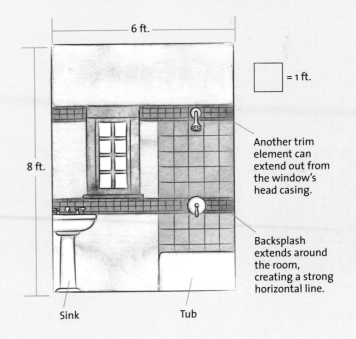

6 ft.

8 ft.

☐ = 1 ft.

Another trim element can extend out from the window's head casing.

Backsplash extends around the room, creating a strong horizontal line.

Sink   Tub

▼ WITH THEIR ROUGH SURFACE and rich earth tones, these 6-in. by 12-in. tumbled slate wall tiles provide a rustic contrast to the contemporary fixtures in this modern bathroom. The warm wood tones introduced by the *iroko* (an African hardwood) vanity are reinforced by the copper wall tiles that are interspersed with the slate and used for the baseboard.

▲ A STUDY IN THE CREATIVE POSSIBILITIES of glass, this contemporary bathroom's 12-in. by 12-in. etched celadon field tiles are interrupted by three different configurations of glass accent tiles. The high-relief glass base molding has a triangular profile and can also be used as crown molding when inverted.

An Exotic Bath in the City

WHEN IT CAME TIME TO RENOVATE the master bathroom in this 1927 Spanish-style Santa Monica, Calif., home, the owners wanted to increase the room's volume and add an Old World touch to the space. Part of the solution was to bump out a wall to create a "wet" room that would include both a soaking tub and an open shower with a steam function.

To keep the wet room from looking too contemporary, Los Angeles designer Lori Erenberg used a line of handcrafted Italian tile that reflected the owner's interests in the art and architecture of France and Italy. Distressed, white 8-in.-sq. field tiles interspersed with blue-and-gold accents cover the floor, walls, and ceiling, creating a moisture-proof environment with the look of an exotic bathhouse. Various sizes and types of decorative tiles—some with Giotto-like portraits, others in checkerboard and floral patterns, and still others in lozenge-like shapes—were used by Erenberg to create floor patterns (see the detail photo) and wall accents that turn the room into a unified and comprehensive composition.

Framed by a marble entryway from the vanity area of the bath and complete with a vintage 1940s-style casement window opening up to a nearby garden, this California bathroom feels as if it would be equally at home on the Adriatic.

◀ ▲ ANTIQUE-LOOKING, HANDCRAFTED ITALIAN TILE gives the wet room in this renovated California bathroom an Old World look, while offering a durable and moisture-resistant finish on the floor, walls, and ceiling.

► TRUE TO ITS MEDITER-
RANEAN HERITAGE, this
home's master bath fea-
tures marble mosaic tiles
covering one wall and act-
ing as wainscoting for the
others, which feature
Venetian plaster. The coordinating 12-in. by 12-in.
giallo marble floor tiles
have pillowed edges and a
honed finish that give the
floor a more aged look.

▲ LIKE A TRADITIONAL
JAPANESE SENTO, this
bathroom uses organic
materials and muted
colors to create a feeling
of serenity and sanctuary.
Randomly patterned,
floor-to-ceiling porcelain
mosaic tiles envelop the
walls with a subtle, soothing texture that con-
tributes to the room's
natural tranquility.

► GREEN, VERMONT SLATE
TILES with a cleft finish,
along with the matching
⁵⁄₄-in. honed slabs on the
countertop and tub deck,
bring beautiful texture
and natural color to this
warm and serene contem-
porary bathroom. Slate
and other porous stones
should always be protected
by a sealer in any wet
environment.

Glass Act

LIKE WALL-MOUNTED GEMSTONES, **glass tiles** seem to radiate color and light. And as any beachcomber worth his or her salt can attest, glass and water have a natural affinity, so the explosion of interest in using glass tile in the bathroom should come as no surprise. Of course, glass is impervious to water, making glass tile a logical choice for tubs and showers, as well as for pools and spas.

Glass tile is also available in an astonishing range of sizes, textures, shapes, and colors. Mosaic tiles, which are typically mounted on 1-sq.-ft. sheets, can be as small as ⅜ in. by ⅜ in. sq., while individual tiles can be as large as 18 in. sq.

With translucency ranging from opaque to transparent, glass tile can be produced with varying degrees of surface texture as well, from mirror smooth to sandpaper rough, and edges can be rounded over or squared off.

While intended primarily for decorative purposes, glass tile that is rated for floor use (when properly installed) is now also available. Price is probably glass tile's only stumbling block: With the exception of one-of-a-kind art tile, glass is the most expensive kind of decorative tile. Expect to pay at least $20 per sq. ft., but don't be surprised to find glass tile in the $200-per-sq.-ft. price range.

▲ GLASS TILE IS MADE IN A VARIETY OF SIZES AND TYPES, including sheet-mounted mosaics, larger field tiles, and decorative borders. A range of transparent, translucent, and opaque colors is also available; metallic glazes are used to give glass tile iridescence.

◀ FIRST INTRODUCED BY ITALIAN GLASS ARTISANS IN THE SIXTEENTH CENTURY, glass mosaic tiles have become more widely available and affordable (though they're still expensive) thanks to recent advances in manufacturing technology. Tiled with ¾-in.-sq. glass mosaics, this bathroom has unique gold mosaic accents created by sandwiching 24-kt. gold leaf between two layers of glass.

Countertops and Backsplashes

IF YOUR BATHROOM HAS A VANITY CABINET, one way to economically incorporate tile into your bathroom's design is with a tile countertop. Because vanities are small and wear and tear is limited, there are more tiling options. Here is where expensive glass or handmade tiles can be used without mortgaging the entire house. Dressing up the sink area and providing your bathroom with a beautiful focal point can be done with just a few square feet of tile.

Often, a tile backsplash is incorporated into the overall design of a bathroom, usually in conjunction with tile wainscot. In a small bathroom, this is a good strategy, as any design that features strong horizontal lines tends to draw the eye outward and create a feeling of spaciousness. And a backsplash also offers the perfect place to get great design bang for your buck, requiring only a small amount of expensive tile to create a rich and compelling look.

▲ ALTHOUGH THESE DECORATIVE TILES create a beautifully textured surface, they'll be more difficult to keep clean than tile with a smooth surface; thus, they're more appropriate in a lightly used powder room than in a family bath.

◄ SMALL, 2-IN.-SQ. TILES with a shiny white glaze introduce an understated textural element to this basic bathroom's countertop, dressing up the space without overpowering it. The simple repeating pattern on the backsplash extends around the room to the tub on the opposite wall, creating a pleasing horizontal element.

▲ IN AN OLD EUROPEAN TECHNIQUE known as *pique assiette,* shards of mirror, fine china, and broken tile (scavenged from estate sales, garage sales, and the discard piles found at most tile showrooms) decorate the top of this powder-room vanity with a curving design inspired by the lines of this old French antique.

◄ THIS CHILDREN'S BATH features bright colors and bold patterns, including a handmade, green-glazed tile countertop with a matte finish. The handmade, blue-glazed floor tile has a glossy finish and uneven texture (to help prevent slips) that suggests water; matching accent tiles are repeated in the backsplash.

▶ MOST PEDESTAL and console-style sinks still need a backsplash to protect the wall from moisture. Here, a wainscot composed of handmade tile featuring a thistle motif does double-duty, protecting the wall above the sink and creating a unifying design element that extends around the room into the shower area.

Color Coordinates

COLOR PREFERENCE is a subjective thing, but there is also an art (if not a science) to choosing colors for a room. Generally speaking, colors toward the red side of the spectrum are considered by many to be warm and exciting, while colors toward the blue side of the spectrum are considered to be cool and calming. Shades of green are considered to be neutral and, like browns and other earth tones, suggest a connection to the land (hence their association with Arts and Crafts–influenced designs).

Because historically the glazing process was unpredictable, tile color trends were influenced to a great degree by glaze chemistry. Blue—a relatively predictable color to create—figures prominently in the tile traditions of a number of countries. Red glazes were more hit-or-miss and are not often found in traditional color palettes.

▲ THIS EXUBERANT SANTA FE BATHROOM'S character comes from its richly detailed tile mosaics and hand-carved cabinetry and woodwork, which are complemented by the more understated colors and patterns of the handcrafted tile used on the countertop and backsplash.

Tub Surrounds

FROM VINTAGE, cast-iron, claw-foot tubs to modern, acrylic whirlpools, there are a wide range of bathtub styles, shapes, and sizes; almost all of them work perfectly with a tile finish. Many bathrooms are still built with a standard 5-ft. tub that does double-duty as a shower. But long before one-piece fiberglass units came to dominate the market, the walls surrounding the tub were almost invariably finished with tile. In a compact bathroom, this is still a great option, and plastic tubs just can't compete with the look and feel of a cast-iron tub surrounded with beautiful tile walls. In larger bathrooms, separate baths and showers allow you to create your own private oasis, a retreat where the day's cares can be soaked away. Choose the kind of soaking tub that perfectly suits your body, and then take advantage of the virtually limitless tile design possibilities to suit your spirit.

▲ THANKS TO THE LARGE ROOF WINDOW and generous mirror over the sink, this San Francisco Bay-area bathroom is filled with natural light. The neutral palette and matte finish of the room's 2-in. by 2-in. tiles help temper the light level and cut down on reflections and glare.

◄ IN THE EARLY TWENTIETH CENTURY, the Arts and Crafts movement flourished in California, and companies such as Muresque Tile in Oakland created distinctive art tile. While most of these companies were done in by the Depression, their beautiful tile remains in installations such as this 1930s bathroom, inspiring the latest renaissance in tile making.

▶ THESE GLAZED, HANDMADE Mexican floor and wall tiles have a high-gloss finish that helps reflect and emphasize the natural light entering this small bathroom from the skylight above. Their rich and irregular texture complements the plaster walls, while their apricot and rust hues imbue the room with nurturing, skin-flattering color.

◀ SOLNHOFEN STONE—a unique German limestone noted for its granite-like strength, smooth cleft surface, and occasional embedded fossil— gives this small monochromatic bathroom subtle texture. Carefully sorted for color and pattern, tiles with the strongest figure were used on the window wall, while more neutral tiles were reserved for the floor.

▼ DEMONSTRATING THE POWER of color and texture to create a feeling of warmth, this sun-drenched bathtub overlooking California's Big Sur is tiled with richly patterned and highly variegated Indian slate. Minimal grout lines emphasize the mosaic of color created by the tile.

▲ INSPIRED BY ITS OWNER'S INTEREST in Islamic art and architecture, this master-bath renovation in a Mediterranean-style, San Francisco Bay-area house features Moorish arches embellished with glass mosaic tile in a design that is light and airy while also cozy and intimate.

▼ THE TRANSITION BETWEEN tiled and non-tiled surfaces needs to be carefully considered when planning an installation to ensure a functional and aesthetically pleasing transition. This arched tub alcove is finished with bullnose and quarter-round trim tiles typical of the 1920s and 1930s.

Tiling on a Budget

IF YOU'RE A BARGAIN HUNTER, you'll be pleased to know that while it's possible to blow your budget on tile, it's also possible to find good deals without having to look too hard. Many tile stores have "bargain basements" where overstocked and discounted tiles are available (though often in limited quantities).

Sometimes manufacturers offer seconds at as low as half the price of their regular tile, while many of the large building-supply chains and home centers have a good selection of tile at bargain prices. And don't forget the Internet; a little sleuthing can yield big rewards, or at least turn up a specific tile that you can't find close to home.

Showers

A WELCOME TREND IN BATHROOM DESIGN is the separation of the shower from the bath. This makes it possible to custom-build larger and safer showers that are better suited to the task than a cramped and slippery enclosed tub. A custom-built shower can be planned to take best advantage of the available space, can include features such as benches and shelves, and can be designed so that it doesn't even require a door.

When selecting tile for a custom shower, start with the floor, choosing a smaller tile, such as an unglazed porcelain mosaic, that can conform to the sloped shower base and that offers good traction. Larger glazed ceramic tile or smoothly polished stone tile are good choices for the walls because they shed soap and clean up easily. Shower walls are a good candidate for decorative tiles, as well, since they tend to be a focal point in the bathroom.

▼ GLASS MOSAIC TILES on the floor, walls, and ceiling of this large bathroom contrast with the smooth, marble tub deck and create a warm texture that nurtures occupants, allowing them to enjoy the generous views without feeling exposed or overwhelmed.

▲ DECORATIVE BORDERS can be composed of a variety of moldings, relief tiles, and other elements and are used to relieve flat planes of tile. This picture rail border helps frame the glass-block window and improves the proportions of the room by giving the impression of a lowered ceiling.

Shower Upgrade

IF YOUR OLD ONE-PIECE, COMBINATION fiberglass tub/shower has seen better days, consider replacing it with a custom-built tile shower. Chances are, your old tub wasn't used for bathing much anyway, and the footprint it occupies is a perfect size for a luxurious shower. The first step is removing the old tub, a relatively easy task because fiberglass tubs (unlike heavy enameled cast-iron tubs) can be cut up into manageable pieces with a reciprocating saw (see the photo below left).

After the old tub has been removed, the space can be prepared for the new shower. This involves modifying the plumbing (for example, moving the drain to the center of the opening and installing a new shower valve), building or installing a waterproof shower pan, and fastening backerboard to the wall (see the photo at right).

Unlike prefabricated showers, site-built showers can be customized to suit your whims and lifestyle. While this, of course, includes your tile selection and overall design, it also can include such personal details as built-in shampoo and soap shelves and seating. Although this kind of upgrade is neither cheap nor easy (costs will vary widely depending on the type of tile you choose but will probably start around $3,500, including labor), it can substantially transform your existing bathroom.

▼ THE INTRODUCTION OF NEW MATERIALS AND ADHESIVES has made preparing an enclosure for a new tile finish a relatively straightforward procedure. Here, cement-based backerboard is fastened to the framing.

▲ AN OLD FIBERGLASS TUB IS A PERFECT CANDIDATE for replacement with a large, tiled, walk-in shower. The best way to remove the old tub is to cut it into manageable pieces with a reciprocating saw after turning off all power and water.

▶ HIGHLIGHTED RATHER THAN HIDDEN by frameless glass doors, this walk-in shower features walls composed of an exquisite, hand-cut, Italian marble mosaic with a wainscot of 3-in. by 6-in., crackle-glazed, hand-made ceramic tile in a running bond pattern. Though separated by a curb and a marble border, the shower floor and bathroom floor are both limestone, which unifies the two areas.

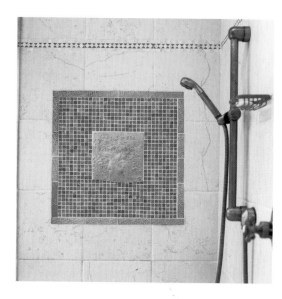

▲ IN A SMALL SHOWER, a relatively petite decorative accent—in this case, a cast-stone medallion surrounded by marble mosaic chiclets and matching cast-stone border—carries a lot of visual weight. The honed marble wall tiles have a satiny texture that softens the light.

▶ MULTIHUED, IRIDESCENT GLASS MOSAIC INSERTS— created by coating the glass tiles with a metallic glaze—almost go unnoticed in this shower, which demonstrates the richness and depth that can be achieved with hand-glazed tiles.

▲ WITH THEIR SLIGHTLY IRREGULAR SHAPE and a surface characteristic of handmade tiles, these 12-in. pavers have a high-temperature, stoneware glaze that reflects and refracts this bathroom's generous natural light, suggesting a Mediterranean ambience of sunlight reflecting on water.

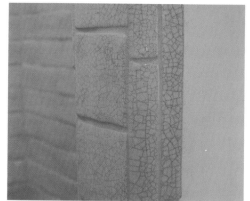

▶ THE RICHLY FIGURED PATTERNS on this crackle-glazed, handmade tile gives the surface depth and invites closer inspection, while the slight irregularities of each individual tile reveal the hand of an artisan.

Photo Finish

WHILE TILE HAS LONG LENT ITSELF to hand-applied decoration, now it's possible to use digital technology to apply photo-realistic images directly onto the surface of various types of porcelain, ceramic, and stone tile. From favorite family photographs to famous artwork, any digital image can be applied either to an individual tile or to a tile mural of virtually any size.

The process involves printing digital images onto special carrier papers using large-format printers and special dye-sublimation inks. These printouts are placed on specially coated tiles, which are then pressure-baked at 400°F. This turns the dyes in the printout from a solid to a gaseous state, allowing them to penetrate the surface of the tile; when the tile cools, the dyes return to a solid state, and the image is permanently transferred to the tile. Because the images are impregnated into the tile surface, these tiles can be used in both interior and exterior applications. (See Resources on p. 152 for ordering information.)

◀ CREATED USING DIGITAL TECHNOLOGY, large-format printers, and special sublimation dyes, photo-realistic murals can be permanently impregnated into the surface of porcelain, ceramic, and travertine tiles. A 4-ft. by 6-ft. mural like this one costs around $2,000.

▶ LIKE THE COORDINATING WALL TILES, these handmade floor tiles are finished with a matte glaze that helps them shed dirt and soap while providing good traction. Their unusual fit—reminiscent of a jigsaw puzzle—offers a unique and unexpected texture and pattern.

◀ ▲ THE ARCHED ENTRYWAY to the shower in this eclectically renovated house is capped by a cast lion's head *voissoir*, the wedge-shaped masonry unit used to form a traditional stone arch. Handmade tiles trim the entry and shower walls, while the floor and baseboard are marble mosaics.

Decorative Accents

AS THE EXAMPLES on the preceding pages illustrate, tile has the power to transform an ordinary room into an extraordinary space. And because most bathrooms are relatively small, even modest details can have a significant visual impact. A diminutive decorative accent in the floor—a rug-like mosaic, for example, or a river-rock border—can be both subtle and surprising. Placing a strategically situated feature on a wall, such as a distinctive molding or a one-of-a-kind mural, can also be used to surprise the eye or create a focal point. Whether your taste in finishing touches runs toward the bold and dramatic or the more understated and subdued, don't be afraid to experiment. Remember, details make the difference.

▶ GLASS ROPE MOLDING FRAMES the doorway into the turret-like spa room of this master bedroom suite, which contains a circular tub finished with amber and black glass tiles. Though the floor looks like terra cotta, it's actually a glazed porcelain tile.

▲ ▶ DECORATIVE, HANDMADE TILES can be expensive, but their cost can be offset by combining them with relatively inexpensive, machine-made field tiles. These tile murals were inspired by magazine advertisements from the 1920s featuring swimmers in Art Deco bathing suits; tile maker Sheryl Murray-Hansen captured their gracefully curved forms in her 3-D tile murals above the bathroom's sinks and tub.

▲ IN ORDER TO REPRODUCE the look of the original bathroom in this restored Hollywood house, an original wallpaper design (taken from a few scraps of remaining wallpaper) was re-created on tile. Ironically, when the wallpaper was first printed in the 1940s, it was a copy of an ornate, Portuguese tile design.

◀ SMOOTHLY POLISHED, washed river rock is available in a range of colors and can be used in conjunction with different types of floor tile to create unique decorative accents and meandering pathways. It can also be used to define transitions or borders between different types of tiles and patterns, as shown here.

▲ THIS WALL SCONCE and the surrounding field and trim tile, made by Muresque Tile in Oakland during the 1930s, are examples of the art and craft of tile making that was practiced in California during the early twentieth century.

Living Spaces

As American families have changed, our homes have changed, too. While there are still houses that are built with separate formal living, dining, and family rooms, more often than not these spaces have been integrated into one interconnected area—a great room—that is open to the kitchen. Sometimes this area may also incorporate a "sunspace," either because the main living area enjoys a favorable southern exposure and ample glass or because there is a separate sunroom adjacent to it.

Whether yours is a home with many rooms or has an open floor plan, these public spaces are where family and friends share time together, and they're well-deserving of surfaces and finishes that are both inspiring and easy to maintain.

Floors, of course, present a perfect canvas for taking full advantage of tile's numerous practical and decorative qualities; with this single material, you can infuse a room with color, pattern, and texture, unify an open floor plan, or distinguish different areas from one another within a larger space. But tile can be used in many other ways, too: focusing attention on a specific architectural element—a fireplace, for example—or adding a decorative accent or a whimsical touch.

As other cultures have long realized, tile is just too good to confine to the kitchen and bathroom. Fortunately, as Americans rediscover the rich traditions and aesthetic attributes of tile, it is making itself more and more at home throughout the house.

◀ CHOSEN TO BALANCE the masculine quality of this home's massive, timber-frame construction and rough-hewn stonework—found both inside and outside the house—blue stone tile with a natural cleft finish was used for the floor. Blue stone also borders the fir strip flooring of the sitting area at the top of the stairs.

Dining Areas and Family Rooms

OPEN FLOOR PLANS—characterized by the integration of living, dining, and kitchen areas—are popular because they recognize the informal way that most families socialize and entertain today. In this type of arrangement, the floor sees nonstop action, so a durable and easily cleaned material, such as tile, that holds up under heavy foot traffic and shrugs off spills makes everyone's life a lot easier. An added bonus is that tile is inert, an important consideration in an energy-efficient home: It doesn't absorb dust, pollen, or other allergens and doesn't off-gas any chemical compounds, making it a better choice for maintaining indoor air quality when a house is relatively airtight. And of course, tile works well with traditional floor plans, too. Use it to enliven a space, add a decorative accent, or simply create a beautiful, low-maintenance floor that enhances your family's lifestyle.

▼ WITH THEIR RICH EARTH TONES and timelessly rustic quality, handmade Mexican Saltillo tiles match the Mediterranean ambience of the dining room in this Spanish colonial home. The tile have been cut into brick-like shapes and laid in a herringbone pattern, suggesting the antique quality of a courtyard.

◄ DESIGNED TO CAPTURE the ruggedness and natural beauty of Maine's rocky coast, this contemporary seaside home features an abundance of concrete offset by the warmth of cedar and cherry woodwork and a radiantly heated Pennsylvania slate floor. The fireplace and hearth is faced with matte-glazed, 8-in.-sq. ceramic tiles and topped with a cast-concrete lintel.

◄ REPRODUCED IN SEPIA TONES from an original antique Flemish tile, this large-scale wall mural of a Viennese horse adds an Old World touch to the atrium of this Santa Fe house.

▲ STRATEGICALLY PLACED ROWS of 4-in.-sq. tiles help break up the sea of larger 8-in.-sq., matte-glazed floor tiles in this oceanside house located on Cape Cod.

DINING AREAS

▶ A FINE-GRAINED, DEEPLY VEINED STONE that is available in a wide variety of colors ranging from black to red to green, slate is an economical and popular flooring choice all around the house. The irregular cleft surface and richly variegated color of these tiles contribute to this dining room's rustic yet refined quality.

▼ AN OCCASIONALLY USED DINING ROOM is often asked to do double-duty, sometimes serving as a computer room or sewing area or—in this case—as the home office for an antique collector. The tile floor's neutral colors and strong pattern add to this room's versatility, standing up well to traffic, contrasting nicely with the wood flooring, and allowing the focus to remain on the furniture.

▲ BUILT WITH VERTICAL-GRAIN FIR, topped with a blue stone slab, and faced with a veneer of Montana ledge stone, this built-in dining buffet matches the rustic character of the rest of the house. The floor is also tiled with blue stone and is radiantly heated.

▲ TILED WITH THE SAME sturdy porcelain tiles used on the kitchen countertops, this simply furnished dining room gets its drama from architectural details, such as the prominent column, the complex ceiling, and the full-height picture windows.

FAMILY ROOMS

▶ WHEN THIS CAPE COD RANCH was renovated with a new second floor, a radiantly heated, terra cotta tile floor was chosen for the living room and kitchen on the main floor. Terra cotta is a good choice for social areas because of its warm, neutral color and durability.

▼ THE NEUTRAL TONE AND LARGE SCALE of these 12-in.-sq., glazed ceramic tiles are a good match for the clean geometry and open floor plan of this contemporary home. An added bonus for this radiantly heated floor is tile's fire resistance, which eliminates the need for a hearth under the woodstove.

What Is Terra Cotta?

PROBABLY THE MOST WIDELY AVAILABLE form of floor tile, terra cotta (literally "cooked earth" in Italian) actually encompasses a number of different colors and types of both handmade and machine-produced tile. At least ½ in. thick (and often more), many terra cottas are fired at a low temperature, making them vitreous and unsuitable for exterior use.

Handmade terra cotta tile is characterized by its irregular shape and texture—finger marks and animal tracks in individual tiles are not unheard of. Terra cotta tiles can also be produced by machine; these extruded or pressed tiles are usually fired at higher temperatures (some are nonvitreous) and are more uniform in color and shape.

◄ ▲ BROWNSTONE IS A RELATIVELY SOFT, sedimentary rock once commonly used as a building material in the decades following the Civil War; here it is used as the flooring for a contemporary condominium. The 12-in.-sq. field tiles are set on the diagonal to complement the irregular configuration of the floor plan, while a decorative mosaic inset, highlighted by accents of Chinese flourite (see detail photo), follows the curve of an interior wall.

▼ PREMOUNTED ON SHEETS for easier handling and installation, stone or ceramic tile mosaics are available in a number of different designs and colors. This simplifies the process of creating and laying out borders and other decorative devices for tile walls and floors.

◄ ▲ WITH ITS SOUTHWESTERN EXPOSURE and convenient access to the rest of the house, this former porch was the perfect candidate for conversion into a combination sunroom/family room. The radiantly heated, quarry tile floor has the look of Mexican tile but is harder and more durable, making it a good choice for indoor/outdoor traffic from the adjacent patio.

◀ AN INTIMATE ALCOVE
that invites reflective
meditation, this Asian-
influenced grotto features
a recirculating fountain,
massive Douglas fir beams
and teak woodwork, and a
radiantly heated blue-
stone floor with an organic
color and rich texture
that's evocative of the
natural world.

Sunspaces

ECAUSE WE'RE DRAWN TO THE HEAT and light of the sun by instinct, many homes feature some sort of sunspace—a solarium, a greenhouse, a conservatory, or simply a room with a lot of south-facing windows—where this most elemental of Mother Nature's gifts can be enjoyed. Besides the spiritual and/or relaxation benefits of a sunspace, a well-designed room can also provide significant energy savings. This is especially true if the floor and/or walls are tiled; because tile is dense, it contributes thermal mass to a room, which helps minimize temperature swings and allows tile-covered surfaces to absorb heat during the day and radiate it at night when the temperature cools down. In addition, tile doesn't fade in the sun, and it can easily stand up to water—especially perfect if the sunspace is devoted to a year-round garden or houses a hot tub or spa.

▲ ANTIQUE TERRA COTTA TILES are being reclaimed from a variety of sources; these have the characteristic honey-brown color of the desert in the Southwest and Mexico and are a perfect complement to the Mission flavor of this California ranch house/retreat.

▶ THIS SUNROOM'S LARGE PORCELAIN FLOOR TILES have a durable, nonslip surface that's fade-resistant and easy to care for. The floor's neutral tone complements the shades of celadon used to decorate the room but would work equally well with a variety of other hues if the homeowners want a change.

▼ THIS SPA ROOM is warmed by radiantly heated, 8-in.-sq., tumbled limestone floor tiles, as well as the sun. Contrasting slab stair treads and baseboards of travertine maintain the room's neutral color scheme while helping to define the stairs and discrete seating areas within the room.

▲ ▶ CUT FROM RECYCLED ROOFING SLATE, the floor of this radiantly heated natatorium has a rough texture and richly variegated color that coordinate well with the space's barn-like, timber-frame construction and the adjoining home's original ashlar stone foundation.

▶ WHILE PERHAPS HARDER TO KEEP CLEAN than a floor covered with darker tiles, the classic black-and-white pattern in this California solarium is a good choice for a warm climate, helping to reflect sunlight, minimize solar gain, and moderate the room's temperature.

▲ BUMPED OUT to take advantage of the sun and the views, this Vermont farmhouse's solar space features a floor tiled with gray and black slate, which absorbs a maximum amount of heat—especially good during the harsh winter. Set in a diagonal pattern, the gray slate helps unify the new space with the existing house.

▶ COUNTERING THE ROOM'S LARGE DIMENSIONS and cool glass surfaces, this radiantly heated, Mexican Saltillo tile floor has a warm, organic color and a richly textured, handmade surface that provides both physical and psychological comfort in the Maine wilderness.

▲ THOUGH SIGNIFICANTLY LESS EXPENSIVE than antique terra cotta, the hexagonal, handcrafted, glazed tiles on the floor of this Maine sunroom have the same warm color and rich French Provincial look in an easier-to-maintain finish.

Fireplaces and Hearths

OLD-FASHIONED FIREPLACES are an architectural anachronism; central-heating systems do a far better job of heating a house and are cleaner and more energy-efficient. But fireplaces have a romantic charm and a proven ability to draw families together as they seek warmth and comfort in front of a crackling fire. Traditional wood-burning fireplaces have long been built with unglazed tiles and bricks and finished with more decorative glazed tiles, all chosen because of tile's fire resistance. These finishes are still popular and can be used to evoke specific architectural styles and periods. Tile treatments can also be used with energy-efficient, gas-fired or wood-burning stoves and modern, zero-clearance prefabricated fireplaces, combining the promise of more economy and better efficiency while helping to evoke the timeless quality of hearth and home.

▲ SMALL BLUE TILES and red plaster face the surface of this minimalist fireplace, built in the style of Mexican architect Luis Barragan, who was known for his adaptation of the traditional materials, architectural forms, and vibrant hues of old Mexico.

◄ DECORATIVE TILES from Moravian Pottery & Tile Works in Doylestown, Penn. —a "living museum" that still creates handmade tile using molds and techniques developed by founder Henry Chapman Mercer in the early twentieth century—give this fireplace an Arts and Crafts touch.

◄ AN INTRICATE MOSAIC composed of cut and ground art glass dresses up the fireplace of this otherwise austere English Tudor home in California. The glass is adhered to three 1-ft. by 4-ft., fire-resistant, cement-based backerboard panels with silicon adhesive, which are then attached directly to the surround.

◄ THE FIREPLACE OF THIS ANTIQUE MAINE CAPE is clad with randomly patterned, 4-in. by 4-in., 4-in. by 8-in., and 8-in. by 8-in. handmade tiles, a more colorful alternative to brick that balances the room's low ceiling with its vertical grid lines. Concrete tiles—some with pewter accents—give the composition a playful, informal quality.

Zero-Clearance Fireplaces

ZERO-CLEARANCE FIREPLACES are an energy-efficient alternative to traditional masonry fireplaces. Prefabricated out of metal with a masonry lining, they're designed to be installed without a foundation or massive chimney and can be configured to burn either wood or gas.

They can be installed virtually anywhere in a house, and options such as automatic thermostats and built-in blowers (used with gas units) make them far more convenient than a traditional fireplace. To keep them looking authentic, tile can be used to trim zero-clearance fireplaces, giving them either a traditional or contemporary feel to suit the architecture of the house.

Historic Hearths

IN THE EYES OF MANY, **the heyday of American tile production occurred early in the twentieth century. This is when companies such as Batchelder Tiles, Rookwood Pottery, and Grueby Faience took to heart the design ideals of the Arts and Crafts movement and created distinctive lines of art tile that celebrated the touch of the artisan's hand. While these tiles, which featured hand-carving, hand-painting, and distinctive glazes, were intended for use all over the house, fireplaces offered a particularly attractive showcase where ideas about materials, workmanship, and unabashed Romanticism that characterized** the English and American Arts and Crafts movement could be synthesized.

Tiled fireplaces play a prominent role in the designs of Charles and Henry Greene, whose California bungalows are perhaps the finest examples of American Arts and Crafts architecture (see the photo below). Many of the same themes embraced by the Arts and Crafts movement more than a century ago—a celebration of handwork as a reaction against technology and an interest in honest materials and expressive details—are popular today and help explain the revived interest in art tile.

▲ A COMBINATION OF ARTS AND CRAFTS STYLE and contemporary technology, this energy-efficient fireplace insert is finished with authentically glazed reproduction tile and a furniture-quality mantel.

◀ THE INGLENOOK IN THE GAMBLE HOUSE, designed by Charles and Henry Greene and built in Pasadena, Calif., in 1908, features generous teak woodwork and a fireplace surround with an intricate art tile design that's inviting to both the eye and the hand.

◀ WITH TWO WALLS OF GLASS, this enclosed porch on a farmhouse in Maine is warmed with the help of a soapstone woodstove and in-floor radiant heating. Adding visual warmth and coziness are the high-fired, handmade stoneware floor and wall tiles in balmy, ocean-side hues of blue and green.

▲ FIREPLACES ARE CHARMING but inefficient, which is why they're often replaced by wood-burning or gas-fired, cast-iron stoves. Delft-style tile, with its roots in the Dutch tradition, has an Old World ambience that makes it a good match for the mantel and helps keep the den of this Maine foursquare bright and cheerful.

◀ THE HAND-PAINTED, black-and-white hunting vignettes on the fireplace surround's tile have a strong graphic quality that complements the rich colors, carved woodwork, and eclectic furnishings of this masculine, Victorian-influenced den.

▲ WITH RICHLY EXUBERANT COLORS and an intricately repeating pattern, the handmade tiles surrounding this unusual fireplace are characteristic of the Mediterranean and Islamic influences on the tile design of California's Arts and Crafts movement.

▶ AN EXAMPLE OF HOW TILE CAN BE USED to help define a style, this room is located in the Casa del Herrero (house of the blacksmith), considered to be one of Montecito, Calif.'s, best-preserved examples of Spanish Colonial Revival architecture. Designed by George Washington Smith in 1925 and remaining virtually unchanged ever since, the estate—now operated as a museum—celebrates the fusion of Mediterranean and Moorish decorative arts.

▲ GOLD TILE—in this case, Bisazza's Oro glass tile, which is a composite of 24-kt. gold leaf sandwiched between two layers of glass—gives this Art Deco fireplace its glitter. Although not a common finish for a fireplace, the use of gold mosaic tile demonstrates how a touch of flash can anchor an otherwise minimalist, modern room with a dramatic focal point.

Fireplace Makeover

ONE WAY TO BREATHE NEW LIFE into an old-fashioned brick fireplace is to face it with tile. This is a relatively straightforward project—well within the capabilities of a competent do-it-yourselfer—that can help transform an ordinary room by taking advantage of the virtually unlimited possibilities of color, pattern, and texture that tile offers. An added bonus is that tiled surfaces are far easier to keep clean than brick.

In this example, the original fireplace, though serviceable, was too small for the rest of the room (see photo at top right). While tile could have been applied directly to it since the masonry was sound, the homeowners decided to have a larger surround framed to better correspond with the scale of the room and to match the new built-in shelving (see the photo at bottom right).

A substrate of cement-based backerboard was attached to the framing to create a new surround and provide a uniform setting surface for the tile. When planning a new surround, be sure to take into account the dimensions of the tile that you will use and carefully plan the tile layout; this helps to eliminate awkward cuts and give the surround a seamless look.

▲ AS IF IT WERE AN AFTERTHOUGHT IN THE ORIGINAL DESIGN, the small, brick-faced fireplace seems out of place in this large room.

▲ NEW FRAMING IS ADDED TO CREATE A LARGER SURROUND FOR THE FIREBOX. A cement-based backerboard will be attached to the framing to provide a smooth and strong setting surface for the new tile.

◄ COLORFULLY GLAZED ITALIAN CERAMIC TILE gives the old fireplace a new look and brightens up the room.

▲ A SIMPLE SURROUND of glazed tile frames this fireplace and introduces an element of color that enhances the woodwork in this small room.

◄ THOUGH PERHAPS AUSTERE by the Victorian standards that were fashionable when this historic Shingle style house—designed by noted Maine architect John Calvin Stevens—was built, this fireplace's surround of glazed relief tile complements the room's intricately carved woodwork and coffered ceiling.

5

Around the House

Though ceramic tile has a 6,000-year history, it's also being reinvented every day. New manufacturing techniques and technologies are being used to create different kinds of tile that could only be imagined a few decades ago. And while decorative tiles—whether exquisitely handcrafted or one of the new manufactured offerings in glass, metal, or other materials—get the lion's share of attention, hard-working tiles intended for everyday use have benefited, too. For example, new glazing processes have been developed that can produce porcelain tiles that look just like natural stone. Tough and virtually maintenance-free, these tiles are perfectly suited for entryways, mudrooms, stairways, and other demanding applications.

All of this innovation has led to new ways of thinking about how tile can be used in the home; offering more options and durability than ever, tile has moved into more industrious rooms such as the laundry. Innovations have also led to a rediscovery of ways in which tile and stone have been used in the past, both within our own recent history and in other eras and by other cultures. For instance, handcrafted art tiles from re-born studios such as Moravian Pottery & Tile Works or Pewabic Pottery remind us of the vitality of our own Arts and Crafts movement, while earth-colored terra cottas and beautiful natural stones keep us connected with ancient traditions from across the globe.

◄ LIKE A WELCOME MAT, pavers patterned to resemble a Persian carpet create an inviting environment in the entryway of this colonial home. An old Mediterranean tradition that invites contemporary reinterpretation, rug-like tile patterns introduce style and texture into a room in enduring colors that are easily maintained.

Entries and Mudrooms

A TRANSITIONAL SPACE LINKING the indoors with the outdoors, entries serve both a functional and symbolic purpose. While creating a welcoming atmosphere for guests and visitors to your home, they should also provide a convenient place for short-term storage of hats, coats, and wet boots. Whether your home's architecture calls for a grand entrance or a more informal welcome, tiled floors and walls are tough enough for the outdoor elements and stylish enough to suit any décor.

If your home is located in a colder climate, you might have (or wish you had) a mudroom. It functions like an airlock, keeping warm air in the house and cold air out, and it provides the perfect place for storing damp or dirty outerwear. Here, industrial-strength finishes are a must, but with tile, you won't have to settle for an industrial look.

▼ RUSTIC BUT NOT PRIMITIVE, this Montana mudroom's slate tile floor matches well with the room's ranch-style wainscoting, which was resawn from logs taken from an old homestead on the property.

▲ A LARGE, SAND-BLASTED GLASS WINDOW, reminiscent of a *shoji* screen, floods the entry—called the "lantern room" by its owners—to this Japanese-influenced home with ambient light, inviting a moment of calm and reflection before entering the main house through the "moongate." Relatively inexpensive, commercial-grade porcelain floor tiles complete the minimalist composition.

▼ A RUG-LIKE TILE PATTERN—created by framing diagonally set Saltillo tiles with a geometric, rectangular border of dark and white tumbled marble—softens this formal entry, while adding an intriguing focal point.

◄ WITH A SMOOTHLY POLISHED, BLACK-AND-WHITE MARBLE FLOOR and vaulted ceiling, this entry foyer is designed for formal entertaining. The five black tiles in the unique, circular floor inset represent family members; the tiles, along with a computer, dictated the layout of the intricate, ten-point star pattern of tile cuts.

▲ IN A HOME WITH AN OPEN FLOOR PLAN, different architectural devices, such as arches or material changes, can be used to define room borders. Here, 16-in.-sq. slate tiles help define the entryway and provide a more durable surface than the adjacent quartersawn white oak flooring that's used in the living areas of this West Coast shingle style house.

▲ POLISHED FRENCH LIMESTONE ON THE FLOORS, stairs, and quoined doorway underneath the stairs contribute to the formal quality of this classically inspired grand entryway, which is framed by a pair of Doric columns.

▶ WITH THEIR CREAMY COLOR AND HONED TEXTURE, the almost randomly patterned limestone floor tiles in this gallery-style entryway provide a subtle counterpoint to the woodwork, while toning down the room's abundant natural light and allowing the visual focus to rest on the surrounding landscape.

◄ A GRANITE SLAB STOOP AND NATURAL BLUE-STONE FLOOR in the entryway provide visitors with a warm greeting at this guest cottage, which is located in the woods at the end of a winding path about ¼-mile from the main house.

▼ ▶ MULTICOLORED SLATE TILES SET IN A HERRINGBONE PATTERN bring an understated element of drama to the entry of this Montana vacation home, which is echoed in the house's service entry (see the detail photo). Highlighted by borders composed of small squares of tumbled slate and glass mosaic tiles, both entryway floors reflect the colors and rugged textures of the Montana landscape while lending a casual elegance to the house.

▲ LARGE 18-IN. BY 18-IN. MEXICAN SALTILLO TILES match the rustic character and massive scale of this log home and extend from the entryway throughout the house. Like most terra cotta floors, the tiles are sealed—in this case with a Mexican glaze that needs periodic reapplication.

◄ THE FOYER OF THIS REMODELED COLONIAL REVIVAL is tiled with limestone that's accented with absolute black granite pin dots. In a nod to the art deco influence that was popular when the house was built, the tile is laid in a diagonal pattern, which adds movement to the circulation space and leads the eye to the living room and vista beyond.

▶ THE ABUNDANT CLASSICAL
REFERENCES IN THIS FORMAL
FOYER are underlined by the
room's tumbled *botticino*
marble floor. Laid in a diagonal pattern to complement
the room's gracefully curving
staircase, the marble has
been finished with a clear
sealer and color enhancer.

Transitions

WHILE IT'S CERTAINLY POSSIBLE **to** use tile as a flooring material throughout a house, in most cases it will be used selectively and in combination with other flooring. This means that part of the process of choosing floor tile is deciding how to handle the transitions between tiled and nontiled floors. In homes with traditional floor plans, this can be as simple as considering doorway details. Usually, some type of low-profile threshold—particularly if there is a slight change in elevation between different flooring materials—is the best way to define and ease the transition (see the top photo).

In homes with open floor plans, logical transitions require a little more planning. For example, a tiled entry foyer, utility area, or passageway may open directly into a living area with a wood floor. Here, a change in elevation between flooring materials is awkward and undesirable, eliminating all but the most subtle threshold styles (see the center photo). Remember, too, that changes in flooring materials can be used to your advantage in an open floor plan; they're one of the devices that can be used to signal where one type of living area begins and another type ends (see the bottom photo).

◀ AN INTRICATE, TRAVERTINE MOSAIC bends around the corner of this foyer, transforming the small floor into a work of art. A simple threshold at the doorway eases the transition between tiled floor and the wood floor beyond.

◀ IN AN OPEN FLOOR PLAN, transitions between tiled and nontiled flooring materials can be dramatic or subtle but should never include a change in elevation. Here, a wood-strip floor and a tiled floor unexpectedly are interwoven in an unusual way.

▶ SLATE SQUARES SET INTO A GRIDWORK OF CHERRY AND YELLOW PINE help define the landing for this staircase and, along with the change in ceiling heights, signal the edge of the living area in this open floor plan.

Decorative Details

IN THE HOT CLIMATE OF THE MEDITERRANEAN, where textile rugs are impractical, the tradition developed of creating intricately patterned and colored, carpet-like designs with floor tile. This tradition was given new life during the heyday of the California Arts and Crafts movement of the 1920s and '30s, which was particularly influenced by Spanish and Italian tile traditions. With the tradition's resurgence in popularity, many tile companies and handcrafters now offer tile lines specifically intended for creating different types of tile rugs in Persian, Turkish, Moroccan, Navajo, and many other styles; numerous examples of these beautiful compositions are scattered throughout this book.

But if a tile rug doesn't fit within the decorative scheme of your entryway (or within your means), there are other ways to embellish a tiled floor that can help you achieve the same personalizing effect. For example, a few strategically placed custom-crafted ceramic inserts can be an effective and economical way to add color, inject a playful mood, or reflect your interests (see the photo at right). Or, instead of a rug, which is bound by the conventional rules of geometry, why not create a tiled pathway that leads you along a meandering path right into the heart of your home? (See the photos below).

▲ IN A HOUSE THAT FEATURES NATURAL MATERIALS AND ORGANIC COLORS, ceramic insets grouted into the bluestone floor create a playful motif, a theme that is repeated in various locations throughout the home.

▲ A TILED, ENTRYWAY FLOOR can be embellished with a few favorite things, like these polished stones and seashells found on the beaches of nearby Cape Cod, as an economical alternative to a full-scale tile "rug."

▲ A LEAFY WALKWAY COMPOSED OF HANDCRAFTED CERAMIC LEAVES ambles through the strip-wood flooring of this entryway, creating a durable path full of year-round color that never needs raking.

▷ A TYPE OF MAJOLICA EARTHENWARE produced since the sixteenth century in the Puebla region of Mexico, these Talavera tiles offer a colorful alternative to wood baseboards and door and window trim in this Spanish-style house. And while the floor looks like authentic terra cotta, it's actually a less expensive and more durable silk-screened porcelain.

◁ A SIMPLE BUT UNUSUAL TILE PATTERN installed with a diagonal orientation gives this entry floor a surprising, not-too-formal twist. Though white tile won't hide dirt as readily as a darker tile, it helps brighten the entry.

▼ ▶ ENTRYWAYS ARE TRANSITIONAL AREAS that connect interior and exterior spaces and help introduce visitors to a home's character. Besides being durable, this entry's natural stone floor has a rugged quality that matches the home's extensive interior woodwork, the antique, recycled chestnut beams that are used both inside and outside of the house, and the fieldstone foundation and landscaping.

Making an Entrance

Most homes have more than one entry, and often the formal front entry is a home's least-utilized space. In that case—or if you do a lot of formal entertaining—style may take precedence over durability and ease of maintenance. But for everyday use, floor and wall finishes should not only be inviting but should also be able to withstand mud, grit, water, and traffic.

Entries are typically small, sparsely furnished rooms, so floor and wall finishes contribute considerably to their design. Don't be afraid of dark colors or bold patterns (as long as they suit your home's architectural style). Entries are transitional spaces, so dramatic elements that may feel overwhelming in a larger room can seem perfectly balanced when you're just passing through.

▼ IRREGULAR SLABS OF ARIZONA ROSE FLAGSTONE suggest colors found in the nearby desert and help brighten the entry of this adobe-style house, which is located on the high plains near Santa Fe, New Mexico.

▲ AVAILABLE IN A WIDE RANGE OF SHAPES AND SIZES, quarry tile is a dense, vitreous tile, making it well suited for high-traffic installations both indoors and out. Most quarry tile is a deep red color, but black and tan tiles are also available.

▲ BECAUSE THE MUDROOM OF THIS PUGET SOUND HOME has direct access to both the garage and a nearby fine-grained pebble beach, the floor gets lots of through-traffic. Slate tile was chosen for both its natural beauty and ability to stand up to tracked-in dirt, grit, and sand.

▶ A LONE CERAMIC FISH INSERT offers a playful touch to the slate floor entryway in this recently built, Shingle-style house. The slate's natural cleft surface keeps the entryway from feeling too formal and reflects the lush, organic surroundings of the rural Maine home.

◄ A FEW EXTRA SQUARE FEET IN THIS HOME'S BACK ENTRANCE make a convenient location for a laundry/mudroom. The floor is covered with large Chinese slate tiles, which have a color and texture that closely match the granite slab countertop over the washer and dryer.

◄ AVAILABLE IN ABUNDANCE THROUGHOUT THE SIERRAS, granite makes an appropriately rugged flooring material for the mudroom/entry of this Lake Tahoe home, which enjoys lots of built-in storage and custom-crafted ironwork detailing.

Stairs and Hallways

WHETHER YOUR HOME'S FLOOR PLAN is open or traditional, each house is made up of living spaces and the circulation patterns that connect them. These are the routes that family members travel on as they pass from one part of the house to another, and depending on the point of origin and the destination, they can qualify as high-traffic areas. If your home has hallways, consider using tile on the floors and walls, both for its durability and its ability to add a discrete or dramatic aesthetic touch to this hard-to-decorate space. Stairways, too, can be dressed up with tile. When used on the risers, just a few tiles can create a unique look that reflects the personality of the house. Or you can opt for a complete tread/riser treatment and enjoy the full benefits of tile's beauty and resilience.

◀ ▲ A FLOOR OF DIAGONALLY SET Mexican Saltillo tiles with occasional insets of smaller, handmade ceramic tiles adds a playful touch to this whimsically informal side entryway. Bordering the floor with a perimeter of square-set tiles defines the entry and helps direct the tile gracefully around the corner into the adjacent hallway (see detail photo).

▼ WITH BRIGHT, TIN-GLAZED COLORS AND BOLD GEOMETRIC PATTERNS that demonstrate the Moorish, Spanish, and Italian influences on their design, hand-painted Mexican Talavera tiles give the risers of this staircase an exuberant Mediterranean look. The terra cotta treads have a rolled edge, making them safer and more comfortable under foot.

▶ TERRA COTTA TILES GET THEIR COLOR FROM THE CLAY where the tiles are produced—primarily Italy and other Mediterranean countries, as well as Mexico—and develop a rich, leather-like patina as they age. Because handmade terra cotta tiles like these are porous, they need to be sealed and periodically maintained.

Step Up to Tile

Found in plazas and palaces throughout Europe, tiled stairways have a long tradition of public service, but their beauty and durability make them a smart luxury in private residences, too. Stair treads should be uniform, with an even surface that offers good traction, so unglazed porcelain or quarry tile makes a good choice. Also available are specially made stair-tread tiles with a rounded nosing.

Risers can be more decorative, and a smooth, glazed surface will make it easier to clean off scuff marks. Riser tile designs can emphasize motifs found on the first floor, or they can be as colorful and whimsical as you like. If your stairway is narrow, a strong horizontal design can make it feel wider; a vertically oriented pattern will emphasize the perception of height in the room.

STAIRS

◀ DECORATED WITH A VARIETY OF DIF-FERENT HANDCRAFTED TILES, these stairs lead up to a tub/shower area. The unusual treads—made up of randomly sized pieces of terra cotta and other types of tile—have a rough, traction-friendly texture that makes them ideal for a potentially wet environment.

▼ COLORFUL, MEDITERRANEAN-INFLUENCED handmade tiles from Malibu Potteries were often used in the construction of Spanish Revival homes like this one in California during the 1920s. While reproductions of Malibu designs are now available, the company itself was forced to close in 1932 after a catastrophic factory fire during the Depression.

▼ AN EXQUISITE EXAMPLE OF ROMANTIC MEDITERRANEAN REVIVAL architecture designed by Los Angeles architect W. Maybury Somervell in 1925, this Spanish colonial home in Montecito, Calif., features a staircase clad with imported Spanish tiles depicting the story of Cervante's *Don Quixote*.

▲ THE RISERS OF THIS SHORT FLIGHT OF STAIRS are tiled with a traditional Islamic pattern that's also found in the famous fourteenth-century Alhambra Palace in Granada, Spain. Adding a dramatic touch in their own right, the tiles also complement other Moorish elements found throughout this contemporary Los Angeles home.

HALLWAYS

▶ SAILING SHIPS ONCE USED DECK-MOUNTED GLASS LENSES to introduce light below decks; here they serve the same purpose (shedding light on a room below), while a channel of small blue tiles helps define a circulation route and connects the dining area with an outdoor fountain.

▼ THIS BASEMENT HALLWAY, which leads to a guest bedroom, is tiled with Mexican terra cotta. While the handmade tiles maintain the monochromatic color scheme, they have an irregular texture that subtly contrasts with the more uniform wall paneling.

▲ WHITE VEINING AND A DEEP RED TINT give these 8-in. by 8-in., *rojo alicante* marble floor tiles—used on a basement hallway leading to a wine cellar—a distinctive Mediterranean flair. The white grout emphasizes the veining and helps define the mosaic border.

◄ HARD, POLISHED SURFACES AND BOLD GEOMETRIC PATTERNS lend a formal, masculine quality to the design of this foyer, which is reflected in its marble and granite floor.

Accessorizing in Tile or Stone

SMALL ARCHITECTURAL DETAILS can make a big difference in a room's overall design. For example, one easy upgrade is to replace standard-issue switch-plate and receptacle covers with higher-quality covers that more closely approximate your home's architecture. While metal covers in brass and stainless steel are common alternatives, ceramic covers in a wide range of styles, colors, and designs are available from a variety of different sources and may be a better match, particularly if handcrafted tiles figure prominently in your design. Likewise, new—and sometimes matching—ceramic cabinet knobs are an effective way to give a set of cabinets a facelift.

It's also possible to complement stone floors with matching switch-plate and receptacle covers. A number of different fabricators, such as Bedrock Stone in California, offer covers in materials such as slate, marble, limestone, granite, and travertine. In addition to standard sizes and switch-plate configurations, most fabricators can produce custom sizes and shapes upon request. And if your stone floor is interrupted by HVAC vents, consider using one of Bedrock Stone's beautiful vent covers, available in a range of sizes in granite, marble, limestone, and slate.

FABRICATED FROM DIFFERENT TYPES OF STONE, including marble, granite, limestone, and slate, these HVAC, switch-plate, and receptacle covers are available in a range of stock and custom sizes and configurations from Bedrock Stone.

Laundry Rooms

WASHING MACHINES AND DRYERS don't take up much floor area, which probably explains why they often end up shoehorned into closets and basements. Fortunately, homeowners and designers are recognizing that a functional, conveniently located space that is dedicated to laundry makes a lot of sense. In a larger house, of course, that space can be a fully equipped laundry room with a deep sink, storage cabinets, and even a utility shower for washing pets. Sometimes situated near the bedrooms on the second floor (where most dirty clothing is generated), laundries can also be logically placed on the ground floor next to a utility entrance. If a separate laundry room is out of the question, laundry spaces can be incorporated into kitchens, pantries, and master bathrooms. With a little creativity—and a little help from tile—these spaces can be both stylish and fully functional.

▲ PETS AND PET OWNERS ALIKE SHOULD FEEL PAMPERED in a laundry like this, which features abundant cabinetry, outside access, a handmade tile countertop, a pet shower finished with a colorful tile mural, and a travertine tile floor.

◀ THOUGH A LAUNDRY ROOM IS A UTILITARIAN AREA, a few simple touches—such as the kitchen-style base cabinet, countertop with stainless-steel laundry sink, and distinctively tiled backsplash shown here—can help dress it up and make the hours spent there folding and sorting clothes less tedious.

▲ DESIGNED FOR WORK RATHER THAN SHOW, this combination pantry/laundry room functions like a second kitchen with plenty of shelving for storage, a working stainless-steel sink, and a low-maintenance, commercial-grade porcelain tile floor that's tough enough to stand up to constant traffic.

▲ CONVENIENTLY LOCATED AT ONE END OF A LONG, GALLEY-STYLE KITCHEN and concealed by simple beadboard cabinetry, the full-service laundry center in this oceanside vacation home is bright and cheerful thanks in part to the room's boldly patterned floor tile.

▶ A PRACTICAL PORCELAIN TILE FLOOR LAID IN A RANDOM PATTERN reflects this laundry room's utilitarian roots, while tumbled, natural slate on the countertops and on the decorative border above the sink reinforce the remodeled ranch home's new, rustic Southwestern décor.

6

Exterior Tile

Because tile is so well suited for kitchens, bathrooms, and other areas inside the house, it's easy to forget that it originally was intended for exterior use. Centuries-old installations of tile still look beautiful, whether crowning the mosques of Tehran, embellishing the gardens of the Alhambra in Granada, Spain, or decorating building façades in Lisbon. These Mediterranean traditions influence many New World decisions about how and where to use tile, and it's not unusual to find imported or reproduction Portuguese *azulejos* or Italian *maiolica* tiles decorating fountains, pools, and gardens in California and Florida.

But whether made of ceramic, stone, or glass, tile's practical and decorative qualities transcend culture and geography. An appropriate tile that has been properly installed can be used to create a unique and durable surface in virtually any style and climate; there is virtually no limit to the ways in which tile can be incorporated into the exterior landscape. Use a few special tiles to transform a stairway or an entryway, for example, or use tile in abundance to create a custom-made, outdoor world. Whether you live on the Maine coast or in the desert Southwest, there is a tile that is perfectly suited for your tastes and landscape.

◀ A FEW HANDCRAFTED TILES WITH AN ORGANIC GREEN GLAZE that reflects the surrounding landscape dress up the stark concrete façade of this outdoor fireplace, giving it an invitingly rustic look that matches the ambience of this outside living room. The pergola overhead provides partial shade and a psychological sense of protection from the elements.

Outdoor Entries

REALTORS CALL IT "CURBSIDE APPEAL": it's the impression that your home imparts to visitors long before they step foot in the front door. A house's architecture plays an important role in making a positive first impression, of course, but it's also the little details that count—for example, a well-designed and maintained front-yard landscape, a welcoming walkway, and an inviting and sheltering entry. This is where a little tile can be used for maximum effect, adding color and character in both traditional and surprising ways. New innovations in ceramic tiles and setting materials add even more options to the palette of traditional stones, pavers, and quarry tiles used for steps and landings. Less exposed to the weather, stairway risers offer an ideal venue for decorative tiles. And a colorful door or window casing of hand-painted tile perfectly complements stucco or adobe construction, providing a finishing flourish to any Southwest or Mediterranean-style home.

▶ A COVERED ENTRY, CALLED A ZAGUAN, connects the guest quarters and the main building of this modest New Mexico hacienda, creating a sheltered area that extends the home's living space to the outdoors. Bricks rated for severe weather cover the entry and step down into the adjacent courtyard.

▲ ▶ FACED WITH THE NECESSITY OF REPAIRING ROTTED WOODEN LINTELS and damaged stucco, the new owners of this 1933 Monterey colonial (see the small photo above for a before shot) gave the entire façade a Spanish Revival facelift. Hand-painted, Mediterranean-influenced tiles frame the openings, while the new mahogany door with hand-forged black iron hardware is sheltered by a new balcony overhead.

▶ TRADITIONAL FORMS ARE GIVEN AN UNEXPECTED, CONTEMPORARY SPIN in this portico-like entry, with Greek-inspired columns framing a tiled entryway. The use of large black tiles instead of colorful Spanish or Italian patterns lends a more formal air to the design.

▲ USED TO DEFINE A DOORWAY (see the photo at left) or to brighten up a set of entry stairs ▲ (see the photo at right), tile adds a splash of color and style to the neutral palette of stucco construction. Handcrafted, glazed tiles like these are best suited for vertical applications in warmer climates, where they are protected from the effects of water intrusion and freeze/thaw cycles.

Steps and Terraces

BESIDES BEING FAR MORE DURABLE AND MAINTENANCE-FREE, a terrace or patio that is clad with a stone or ceramic tile has a solid, timeless quality that you just can't get with a wooden deck. An addition to various types of stone, high-fired and frost-resistant quarry tiles, porcelain, terra cotta, and even glazed ceramic tiles can all be used in a wide range of climates to create understated or dramatic outdoor "rooms" that are rich combinations of pattern and color. Steps offer the same opportunity but on a far smaller (and more economical) scale. Pavers made of high-fired terra cotta, porcelain, or vitreous quarry tile are great choices for treads, while more colorful tiles—even glazed decorative tiles in traditional Mexican or Mediterranean styles—can be used to brighten up the vertical surface of the risers.

▲ BITS AND PIECES OF STONE, GLASS, AND CERAMIC TILE—some placed upside down— add color and texture to this spiral steel staircase. The fragments are embedded in mortar, giving the treads a smooth, safe surface to walk on.

▲ IN-FLOOR RADIANT HEATING MEANS NEVER HAVING TO SHOVEL SNOW off this second-story deck overlooking Maine's Penobscot Bay. Suitable for outdoor use even in coastal Maine's harsh climate, the deck's through-bodied porcelain, 12-in. by 12-in. tiles have an unglazed, natural stone-type finish and are impervious to moisture.

◀ WHEN THE NEGLECTED AND ONCE-BURIED ENTRY STAIRWAY of this historic 1928 Spanish Revival villa was rebuilt, the risers were faced with reproductions of Moorish-influenced Portuguese tile. Because of their similar sunny and mild climates, both the Mediterranean and Southern California are well suited to the use of all kinds of tile in exterior settings.

◀ ▲ STURDY MEXICAN PAVER TREADS
PROVIDE GOOD TRACTION for these
stucco staircases, while the risers,
which are covered with handcrafted
tiles glazed in vivid colors and abstract
forms, provide an exuberant Southwest flavor along with the custom-
fabricated, wrought ironwork.

▲ ▶ **LIKE THE ANDALUSIAN** *CORTIJOS* (rural manor houses and farmhouses) of southern Spain that inspired its design, this 1920s Los Angeles home features a courtyard terrace that figures prominently as one of the house's central living areas. Thick Mexican paver tiles contribute to this outdoor living room's rustic charm, while a small fountain tiled with colorful, Portuguese-style tile (see the photo above) adds the soothing sound of splashing water, an important courtyard element in the hot, dry cultures of the Mediterranean...and California.

◀ PAVERS CUT FROM MEXICAN PORPHYRY—a very hard volcanic rock favored by the Egyptians and Romans for its strength and durability—cover the courtyard and steps of this Southwest adobe home. A popular European building stone, porphyry gets its name from the Greek word *porphyros* (for the color purple).

▲ CHOSEN FOR ITS SMOOTH SURFACE (for use under terrace furniture) and its natural connection to the historic stone house in New York's Dutchess County, this bluestone terrace was dry-laid with stone dust and then sealed to deepen its color and prevent moisture damage.

Exterior Tile Choices

CHOOSE OUTDOOR TILES with a slip-resistant, textured surface for stairs, terraces, and patios. Unglazed ceramic tiles, such as Mexican Saltillo pavers or Italian or French terra cotta tiles, are traditional choices, though their relatively soft, low-fired clay bodies will show more wear and tear than a harder unglazed porcelain tile. Other good options are quarry tile, smaller tiles with numerous grout lines, and natural stones with cleft or honed surfaces. There are also many new tiles intended for outdoor use that have abrasive particles actually incorporated into their surface. They are stronger, thinner, and sleeker than traditional tiles, and are available in a wide range of textures, sizes, shapes, and colors.

Indoor/Outdoor Spaces

OUR TECHNOLOGICAL WORLD is a complex one, but when it comes right down to it, the essential ingredients—air, earth, fire, and water—are all that we really need. Outdoor spaces fill that need, offering a cooling breeze, the warmth of the sun, a place to garden, or the sound of splashing water to soothe and refresh our spirits. Tile can be used in a variety of ways to help create and transform outdoor spaces, whether as an understated flooring material or as a dramatic vertical element that dresses up outdoor barbecues, garden walls, or fireplaces. Whether your landscaping plans call for a few simple touches or an elaborate exterior environment, there is a stone, ceramic, or glass tile that is well suited to your design.

▲ PERCHED ON THE SECOND FLOOR FOR PRIVACY, this porch on a Houston home has an eastern exposure to take advantage of the morning sun but provides shade from the hot Texas afternoons. The floor is covered with honed slate to match the flooring used in the master bath.

◄ SET INTO A SURROUNDING FLAGSTONE PATIO, this small soaking spa is lined with blue-glazed ceramic tile that gives the water rich color and the illusion of depth, while providing a stain-resistant surface that's easy to keep clean. Because even Santa Barbara, Calif., occasionally has inclement weather, the glass enclosure keeps occupants warm but has a minimal impact on the view.

▶ THE FRONT VERANDA OF THIS GREENE & GREENE-DESIGNED HOME overlooks the front yard and gardens, offering cool refuge from Pasadena's mid-summer heat. It was recently refloored with unassuming, brick-colored porcelain tiles in a simple pattern that doesn't detract from the home's original Arts and Crafts detailing.

◀ THIS LOGGIA IS DESIGNED FOR CONTEMPORARY OUT-DOOR LIVING, with a built-in grill and durable stone tile surfaces on the floor, walls, and ceiling. Changes in floor-tile size and pattern add interest to the floor and help define sitting areas vs. work areas within the larger space.

▲ A DENSE, FINE-GRAINED SANDSTONE THAT SPLITS READILY into relatively smooth-faced thin slabs, bluestone (which is actually available in colors ranging from brown to green to lilac in addition to blue) is well suited for use both inside and outside the home. Here, random sizes have been dry-laid on a stone dust base (with no mortar or grout).

▲ DECORATED WITH METICULOUSLY HAND-PAINTED REPRODUCTION TILE MURALS, this grand fountain welcomes visitors to a Portuguese-style *quinta* (or manor house) located in Montecito, California. Tile makers in eighteenth-century Portugal were clearly influenced by the Dutch tin-glazed tradition—Delft tile is a good example—but their blue-and-white *azulejos* murals tended to be executed in large scale rather than on individual tiles.

Under the Weather

WATER IS RELENTLESS. It can work its way through hairline cracks and soak into porous surfaces and then expand when it freezes, causing tile to chip, crack, or work loose. Unless you live in a warm climate that doesn't experience any freezing, choose tile for your landscape that is vitreous or impervious and has been rated as frost-resistant and suitable for exterior use. This can include high-fired quarry tiles and impervious porcelain pavers, as well as some glazed tiles (be sure to check for a specific recommendation from the manufacturer). In warmer climates, save fragile decorative tiles for use on vertical surfaces, where they can more easily shed water.

▲ USED EXTENSIVELY FOR THE EXTERIOR LANDSCAPING of this Martha's Vineyard home, bluestone makes a natural transition to the indoors and is used to help create a comfortably sheltered screened porch that's perfect for enjoying summer's cooling breezes

Water Structures

WHETHER THE SETTING IS A BROOK splashing down over rocks or an intimate pool that quietly reflects the surrounding landscape, water commands our attention. Water structures placed in the landscape—anything from a small fountain to a full-size pool—help capture those sights, sounds, and sensations that draw us so powerfully to water, creating a private backyard oasis. Add tile to the equation, and the effect becomes even more magical; water becomes eternally blue in the presence of blue tile, even when the skies are overcast, while colors seem to shimmer and intensify, especially when splashed with sunlight. And tile is a practical choice, too. Four to 6 in. of tile placed along the waterline of a pool, for example, helps resist the accumulation of mineral deposits and dirt that might otherwise occur as water levels fluctuate due to evaporation.

▶ THIS FOUNTAIN IS PART OF A MASSIVE RETAINING WALL that includes a curving staircase. The handcrafted tile that lines the fountain was inspired by the colors and style of art tile produced by Malibu Potteries in the 1920s.

▼ THE CENTER OF ATTENTION IN A SPANISH-STYLE SOUTHERN CALIFORNIA COURTYARD, this fountain's colorful, Tunisian-style tile is hand-painted with the traditional colors and intricate patterns characteristic of Moorish design.

▲ WATER SPILLS OVER THE EDGES OF THIS SMALL MARBLE FOUNTAIN and falls into a stone-edged and pebble-lined rill, which circulates it through the surrounding California citrus garden. Traditional, hand-cut and hand-painted Moroccan *zeligge* mosaic tiles line the bottom of the fountain, while the spout is carved from alabaster.

◄ ► COLORFUL, HANDMADE MOSAIC TILES bring a playful taste of Tahiti to this California pool and spa. Because they shed mineral deposits, resist fading, and are easier to clean than concrete, glazed tiles are a good choice for pool and spa waterlines.

▲ HAND-GLAZED ITALIAN CERAMIC TILES DECORATE THE SPA AND BARBECUE that flank the sides of this Vermont pool. While the pool deck looks like natural stone, it is actually concrete that has been factory-colored and stamped after being poured, giving it stone-like texture and pattern.

▲ BECAUSE GLASS IS IMPERVIOUS TO MOISTURE, these glass tile mosaics are highly stain-resistant and frost-proof, making them a good choice for swimming pools in all climates. Available in a wide range of colors, glass tile also won't fade when exposed to UV light.

▶ GENEROUSLY SIZED DOORS AND WINDOWS can totally enclose this courtyard, creating a year-round retreat in this Pacific Northwest home. The courtyard features a small, resistance-style exercise pool surrounded by porcelain tiles in a neutral color, which complement the natural look of the split-faced, concrete block walls as well as those done in cedar plywood-and-batten.

▲ ENCLOSED BY A CIRCULAR HEDGE AND SURROUNDED BY A GROVE OF BIRCH TREES AND A PERENNIAL GARDEN, this private spa offers refuge from the summertime crowds on Martha's Vineyard. The gunite spa is trimmed with gray slate tiles and surrounded by a bluestone terrace that offers understated elegance and a slip-resistant surface.

Choosing Pool Tile

POOLS, SPAS, AND FOUNTAINS require vitreous or impervious tiles that won't absorb water and that resist chemicals and fading. A row of smoothly glazed tiles at the waterline will shed dirt more easily than concrete, making the pool easier to keep clean, while matte-finished tiles provide better traction and are more appropriate for steps, seating, and floors. It's generally impractical to tile an entire swimming pool, but accents inset into the floor and walls can have a strong visual effect. A standard size for pool tile is 6 in. square, but other shapes and sizes are available; use paper or mesh-mounted mosaics in glass or ceramic tile to conform to curved surfaces.

▲ THE SMALL FOUNTAIN THAT HELPS DEFINE THE EDGE OF THIS CALI-
FORNIA COURTYARD is built with cinder blocks and finished with
stucco. Handmade, blue-glazed tiles line the interior, giving the
pool its deep blue color, while a few strategically placed hand-
painted accent tiles give the fountain its Mediterranean look
without breaking the bank.

◄ A QUIET REFLECTING POOL CREATES
A SERENE MOOD IN THIS SPANISH-STYLE
COURTYARD. The honed stone tiles surrounding the pool are divided into four-
tile grids with thin bands of contrasting
stone, creating the illusion that the
courtyard is surfaced with massive
stone slabs.

▲ INSPIRED BY TRADITIONAL SPANISH-
TILED "BLANKETS" used to decorate
stucco building façades, this fountain's
undulating design seems to shake right
out of the wall, giving it a dimensional
quality. Covered with handcrafted tiles,
the fountain is flanked on both sides by
planters topped with Mexican pavers.

▲ DESIGNED TO MATCH THE ANDALUSIAN STYLE OF THIS 1929 Beverly Hills home, a new combination fountain/reflecting pool was lined with colorful Spanish tile to give the water a rich hue and the illusion of depth.

Decorative Accents

▲ A SIMPLE WAY TO DRESS UP CLAY POTS AND PLANTERS is to decorate them with washed stones, bits and pieces of tile or pottery, or other small objects that are glued on with marine-grade adhesive. A good source for ceramic shards are the discard piles found at most tile showrooms.

B ECAUSE OF THE SHEER SCALE of an exterior landscape, tile is most often used as a decorative accent rather than as a primary finish material. Examples on the previous pages demonstrate how a few tiles used as door or window trim can help create architectural interest on an otherwise plain building façade. The same strategy can be employed on landscaping elements such as fireplaces or garden walls, forming focal points or splashes of year-round color that brighten up otherwise neutral masonry surfaces. Thoughtful placement of these accents and focal points will make them visible from inside the home, too, creating vistas that draw the eye out into the landscape. Tile can be a moveable feast, as well. Use it imaginatively on furniture, planters, and other accessories, taking advantage of its beauty and durability the whole year through, both inside and outside the house.

▲ WITH A TILED TABLETOP, you can experiment with ceramic colors and styles on a small scale, matching the existing surroundings or going off on a totally different tangent. Best of all, this is a work of art that you can take with you, from season to season or from house to house.

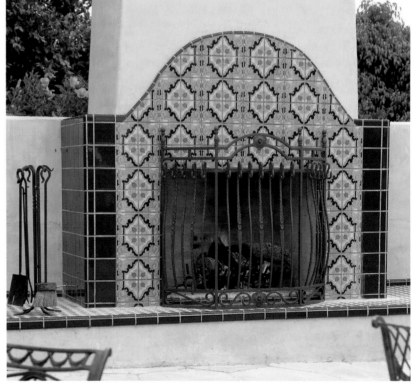

▲ DURING THE 1920s AND '30s, tiles from Malibu Potteries were noted for their vivid colors and Moorish and Tunisian-influenced designs, characteristics that have made contemporary reproductions—like those found on this garden fireplace—popular once again.

◀ ▲ TILE BY HAND-PAINTED TILE, the story of *Don Quixote* is told in this lovely ceramic series that extends across the base of this outdoor fireplace and around the courtyard of a Spanish Revival-style house built during the heyday of 1920s Hollywood.

Resources

Busby-Gilbert Custom Tile
16021 Arminta Street
Van Nuys, CA 91406
818-780-9460
www.busbygilberttile.com

California Potteries
859 East 60th Street
Los Angeles, CA 90001
323-235-4151

Ceramica Specialty Tiles
2504 West Main Street
Bozeman, MT 59718
406-582-8989

Colleen Horner/Kitchen-Bath-
Tile-Stone
191 North Broadway
Milwaukee, WI 53202
414-298-9969
www.colleenhorner.com

Crossville Porcelain Stone
P.O. Box 1168
Crossville, TN 38557
800-221-9093
www.crossvilleinc.com

Eco Ceramica Tiles
Via D. Pio Borghi, 5
S. Antonio Di Casalgrande
Reggio Enilia, (RE), Italy, 42010
011-390-536-990177
www.ecoceramica.com

European Bath Kitchen Tile &
Stone
143 South Cedros
Solana Beach, CA 92075
858-792-1542

Gustin Ceramics
231 Horseneck Road
South Dartmouth, MA 02748
508-636-6213
www.gustinceramics.com

Harbor Farm
Route 15
Little Deer Isle, ME 04650
207-348-7737
www.harborfarm.com

Images in Tile
P.O. Box 19750
Denver, CO 80219
303-922-4007
www.imagesintile.com

Lascaux Tile Works
P.O. Box 48376
Los Angeles, CA 90048
323-939-6039

M.E. Tile Co., Inc.
6463 Waveland Avenue
Hammond, IN 46320
708-210-3229
www.metile.com

Michelle Griffoul Studios
84 Industrial Way
P.O. Box 1149
Buellton, CA 93427
805-688-9631
www.michellegriffoul.com

Moravian Pottery & Tile Works
130 Swamp Road
Doylestown, PA 18901
215-345-6722

Morningstar Marble &
Granite, Inc.
47 Park Drive
Topsham, ME 04086
207-725-7309
www.morningstarmarble.com

Oceanside Glasstile
2293 Cosmos Court
Carlsbad, CA 92009
866-648-8453
www.glasstile.com

Paragon Tile & Stone, Inc.
P.O. Box 230845
Tigard, OR 97281
503-684-5330
www.paragontile.com

Pébéo
305, Avenue de Bertagne
BP 106 – 13881 Gémenos
Cedex, France
www.pebeo.com

Romano Tile Installation, Inc.
325 Lunt Road
Brunswick, ME O4011
207-798-6682

Solnhofen Natural Stone, Inc.
1604 17th Street
San Francisco, CA 94107
415-552-1500
www.solnhofen.com

SwimEx Systems
373 Market Street
Warren, RI 02885-0328
800-877-7946
www.swimex.com

Tedeschi Tile and Marble, Inc.
1232 East Main Street
Torrington, CT 06790
860-489-7463

Tek Tile
72 Acacia
Orinda, CA 94563
925-330-2148

Tile Showcase
Suite 639,
One Design Center Place
Boston, MA 02210
617-426-6515
www.tileshowcase.com

Tileworks of Westminster West
3400 Westminster West Road
RFD 3 Box 728
Putney, VT 05346
802-387-6661

Credits